Social Ministry in the Lutheran Tradition

Social Ministry
in the
Lutheran Tradition

edited by
Foster R. McCurley

Fortress Press
Minneapolis

SOCIAL MINISTRY IN THE LUTHERAN TRADITION

Cover art: Detail from *The Last Supper and Washing of Feet.*
Insets from top: (1) *The Last Supper and Washing of Feet*, detail from Baptistery, Florence, Italy, 13th century. Photo © Erich Lessing /Art Resource, NY; (2) *Second Work of Mercy: Reception of the Pilgrim in His House*, woodcut by Albrecht Dürer; (3) Inuit church women's group, Nome, Alaska. Photo © ELCA Region 3 Archives. Used by permission; (4) photo © Melissa Ramirez Cooper, used by permission.

Cover design: Ivy Palmer Skrade
Book design: Zan Ceeley, Trio Bookworks

Library of Congress Cataloging-in-Publication Data

Social ministry in the Lutheran tradition / Foster McCurley, editor.
p. cm.
Includes bibliographical references and index.
ISBN 978-0-8006-2129-2 (alk. paper)
1. Lutheran Church—Charities—History. 2. Christian sociology—Lutheran Church—History. 3. Social service—Religious aspects—Lutheran Church—History. I. McCurley, Foster R.
BX8074.B4S58 2008
261.8088'2841—dc22

2008011514

The paper used in this publication meets the minimum requirements of American National Standard for Information Sciences — Permanence of Paper for Printed Library Materials, ANSI Z329.48-1984.

Manufactured in Canada

12 11 10 09 08 1 2 3 4 5 6 7 8 9 10

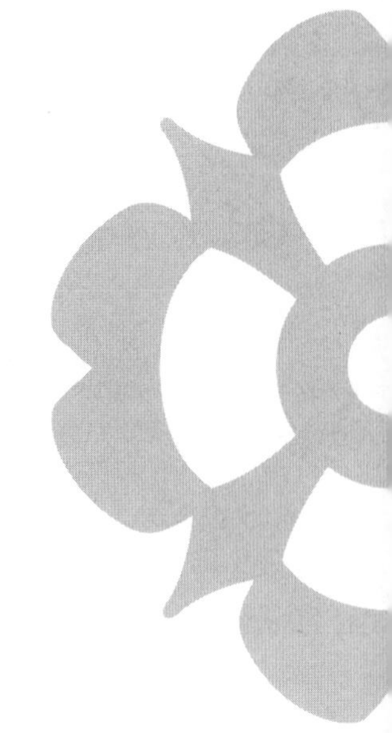

Contents

Editor's Preface

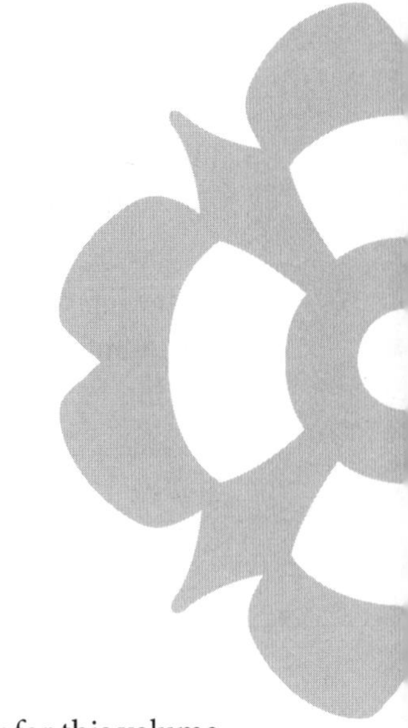

The invitation from Fortress Press to serve as the editor for this volume on justice and social ministry offered me the opportunity to reflect on my own life and ministry and on the church of which I have been a member since my baptism as an infant. Joining others in writing these chapters enabled me to celebrate anew the community of faith that nurtures us all and binds us in a commitment to serve our neighbors.

My father used to say, "Son, it's no sin to be poor. It's just hard." Dad was a coal miner most of his life. He saw very little of the light of day. He continually breathed in the dust particles and gases that would eventually cause his death. Because of layoffs, shutdowns, and strikes, his paychecks were meager and inconsistent. His own experience gave credibility to his theological teaching that it is no sin to be poor and to his understatement that life for the poor is hard.

For some totally incomprehensible reason, upon completion of my seminary degree and my ordination, I studied Assyriology in my doctoral program while beginning a two-decade career as a seminary teacher. At the time, I justified the study of cuneiform as a means to better understand the Hebrew language and the Hebrew Bible, which I was teaching. Perhaps the lure of the esoteric inspired me. Whatever the initial motivation, I could not have imagined that this intellectual pursuit of studying the cultures of the ancient Near East, learning their wisdom, and probing their myths and legends would enable me to understand more profoundly the difference between their gods and the God of the Bible. The ancient teachings and myths aimed at justifying the power of the present king or pharaoh or dynasty by identifying his position as the god's image on earth and by asserting this divine supremacy over an entire population of slaves. By contrast, the God of the Bible revealed a different identity—one that is intimately bound up with the poor and the oppressed, one who loves justice and risks divine reputation by making unconditional promises to society's outcasts.

Admittedly, I was slow in learning that the gospel of Jesus Christ in which I had grown up was precisely the good news about a God who was decidedly different from the power and control of the gods who would govern us. Luther's theology of the cross became for me more and more the only way to understand who God is and what it means to live realistically, servingly, and hopefully. That growing realization led me to spend most of the past twenty-five years in ministries focused on justice and social ministry.

In 1988, just as the Evangelical Lutheran Church in America was forming by the merger of two predecessor church bodies, the new Division for Social Ministry Organizations invited me to write a book that might serve as a guide until the new church had opportunities to develop its documents and policies. The process for conducting my research involved on-site visits and interviews with staff and boards of seven Lutheran social ministry organizations in the eastern and midwestern United States. At the end of each visit, I expressed the wish that I could have brought along groups of congregational members to witness, as I did, what exciting ministries the church of Jesus Christ was performing through these organizations.

Over its two decades the ELCA developed a commitment to justice and social ministry that is integrated through its every expression—churchwide units, synods, congregations, and pastors. This church's Constitution admirably grows through changes and additions to define its purposes and functions in light of new realities and opportunities. The ELCA defines its participation in God's mission to a broken world by asserting it shall "serve in response to God's love to meet human needs, caring for the sick and the aged, advocating dignity and justice for all people, working for peace and reconciliation among the nations, and standing with the poor and the powerless and committing itself to their needs" (Constitution of the ELCA [2007], 4.02.c).

Fulfilling this purpose, the church shall "lift its voice in concord and work in concert with forces for good, to serve humanity, cooperating with church and other groups participating in activities that promote justice, relieve misery, and reconcile the estranged" (4.03.g). Further, it shall "study social issues and trends, work to discover the causes of oppression and injustice, and develop programs of ministry and advocacy to further human dignity, freedom, justice, and peace in the world" (4.03.l).

The ELCA exercises these commitments to social justice and solidarity with the poor through the public speaking of its ordained ministers (7.31.12.7), its congregations (9.41.f), its synods (10.21.o), and its churchwide organizations (11.21.d, i). While the social justice responsibilities appear in the list of functions among most of the churchwide units, the focus of this commitment lies in the Church in Society Unit (16.12.DO6).

While the ELCA defines itself as created and sustained by the cross of Christ, the same cross directs its participation in God's mission to a broken world. That commitment to justice and care of the neighbor is so consistent and integral to the ELCA that a reader of its Constitution cannot escape the conclusion that service to the world is the inevitable response to the gospel of Jesus Christ.

The Lutheran Church–Missouri Synod also considers ministry to the suffering of the world to be integral to the gospel. Focusing this ministry through its World Relief and Human Care, the church seeks "to alleviate human suffering and elevate the human condition by responding to emergency and enabling struggling people to become self-sufficient" (from the website www.lcms.org). The theological foundation for this service appears in the following words:

> Love, care and concern for those in need (diakonic mercy / love) are actions motivated by the gospel, when faith (*fides qua creditur* / the faith by which we believe) apprehends the righteousness of Christ and his merits (Augsburg Confession IV & VI), unto eternal life. The gospel thus laid hold of, produces love. Love seeks and serves the neighbor.
>
> Love for the neighbor, while an action mandated by the law of God, is a reflection of the very being of the Triune God, Father, Son and Holy Spirit (I Jn. 4:7). This love finds its source and motivation in the deep gospel matrix and totality of the true faith (*fides quae creditur*/ the faith which is believed).

The LCMS recognizes that "the vocation to mercy is addressed to the church at all levels. The vocation to diakonic love and mercy is as broad as the need of the neighbor (Luther). While the call to love the needy applies to Christian individuals as such (Love your neighbor as yourself), the call to diakonic mercy is particularly addressed to Christians as a corporate community (church!), whether local or synodical, even national or international (I Cor. 16:1-4; Acts 11:28; Rom. 15:26; II Cor. 8:1-15; Acts 24:17)."

The story of the partnering of the Evangelical Lutheran Church in America and the Lutheran Church–Missouri Synod to form Lutheran Services in America is told several times in this book. Both churches have invested themselves heavily in this comprehensive system for human services. Together they witness to the gospel of Jesus Christ through their service and their advocacy.

The people who have joined me in preparing this volume demonstrate the vitality of their dedication to the larger Lutheran church and its commitment to social justice. With astonishingly brief time for preparing, the authors of the chapters devoted their distinctive talents to this project. I owe much gratitude to Samuel Torvend, Carter Lindberg, Eric Gritsch, Carl Uehling, and Robert Duea for their willingness to compose their various insights and to Martin E. Marty for permission to use his essay as the epilogue. I am grateful to the Future's Group for initiating this project and for its discussion that became the final chapter of the book. I am indebted to my wife, Jannine, for her endless hours of work to help with the editing of all this material.

Above all, I am grateful that I am a member of a church that confirms what my father taught me. It is indeed no sin to be poor. But it is God's forgiveness of our sin that enables us to identify with and serve the poor in the pursuit of justice.

About the Contributors

The Reverend Robert Duea served as president and CEO of Lutheran Social Services of Wisconsin and Upper Michigan for the final eighteen of his thirty-three years within the Lutheran social ministry system. Prior to Wisconsin, he served as executive of Lutheran Family Services of Oregon and Southwest Washington and as regional director for Lutheran Social Services of Minnesota. A graduate of St. Olaf College and Luther Seminary, he has continued to be active following retirement, serving in three interim CEO positions for national nonprofit associations as well as providing consulting services for Lutheran Services in America and Arizona State University's Center for Nonprofit Leadership and Management. He and his wife, Marilyn, live in the Phoenix area.

The Reverend Eric W. Gritsch, Ph.D., is Emeritus Professor of Church History at Gettysburg Lutheran Seminary. A native of Austria, he studied at the universities of Vienna, Zurich, Basel, and Yale (Ph.D.) and is the author or co-author of eleven books on Luther and Lutheranism, such as *A History of Lutheranism* (Fortress Press, 2002), *Fortress Introduction to Lutheranism* (Fortress Press, 1994) and *The Wit of Martin Luther* (Fortress Press, 2006). Dr. Gritsch edited nine books, including *Church and Ministry III* in the Luther's Works series (Fortress Press and Concordia Publishing House, 1966). He also translated four books, including Heinrich Bornkamm's *Luther and the Old Testament* (Fortress Press, 1969). He now lives in Baltimore.

CARTER LINDBERG, Ph.D., is Professor Emeritus of Church History, Boston University School of Theology. He holds degrees from Augustana College (Illinois), Lutheran School of Theology (Chicago), and the University of Iowa. Lindberg's most recent works are *Love: A Brief History through Western Christianity* (Blackwell, 2008) and *A Brief History of Christianity* (Blackwell, 2006). He is presently revising *The European Reformations* (Blackwell, 1996) for its second edition. His major interests are Luther studies and the history of Christian contributions to social welfare. He and his wife, Alice, live in the Boston area.

THE REVEREND FOSTER R. MCCURLEY, Ph.D., retired in 2004 from the interim position of president/CEO of LUTHERCARE, a social ministry organization in south central Pennsylvania. Earlier he served as theologian for three social ministry organizations and for the board of Lutheran Services in America. McCurley taught Old Testament and Hebrew for two decades at the Lutheran Theological Seminary in Philadelphia. Among his books is *Go in Peace, Serve the Lord: The Social Ministry of the Church* (ELCA, 2000). Recently his book *Ancient Myths and Biblical Faith* was republished (Fortress Press, 2007). He and his wife, Jannine, and live in Pennsylvania.

SAMUEL TORVEND is Associate Professor of the History of Christianity and Chair of the Religion Department at Pacific Lutheran University (Tacoma, Washington). Dr. Torvend's research focuses on the relationship between sacraments and social ethics in the history of Christianity. In 2004, he was recognized publicly for his work on Lutheran responses to hunger and poverty in Washington State and by the Luther Institute of Washington, DC. Dr. Torvend is the author of *Daily Bread, Holy Meal: Opening the Gifts of Holy Communion* (Augsburg Fortress, 2004) and the forthcoming *Luther and the Hungry Poor: Gathered Fragments* (Fortress Press, 2008). He holds a bachelor's degree from Pacific Lutheran University, a master's of divinity from Wartburg Seminary, a master's of arts degree from Aquinas Institute of Theology, and a doctorate from Saint Louis University.

THE REVEREND CARL T. UEHLING lives in retirement with his wife, Jean, on an old farm in northwestern Pennsylvania. A graduate of Gettysburg College and the Lutheran Theological Seminary at Gettysburg, he also studied at Union Theological Seminary, Columbia University, and Temple University. He served five different congregations, and for ten years he was the articles editor for the *Lutheran* magazine. His books include *Hope and Healing*, a brief history of Lutheran social ministry organizations (Lutheran Service in America, 1999).

1

The Identity and Work of God

Social Justice in the Bible

Foster R. McCurley

The biblical foundation for social justice grows—like the Bible itself—out of the Word of God. As formal and static as that phrase might sound to modern ears, the Word is God's encounter with people. The Word is so dynamic that it accomplishes what it says, even while God is saying it.

We Christians speak of "the gospel of Jesus Christ" as the defining expression of God's Word. The "good news" is about who Jesus is and about what God accomplished in his life, death, and resurrection. Divine identity and divine action erupt from the Word. The same is true of God's Word in the Hebrew Scriptures, Jesus' Bible. The Word delivered through preachers, teachers, and writers informs the questions "Who is the Lord our God?" and "What does our God do that makes the Lord distinct from all other gods?"

The answers to such questions can come only from God. God announced what the people could not comprehend on their own. This divine self-revelation of identity and action came to the people of Israel through Moses and the prophets. God's revealing of the identity and work of Jesus came through the Spirit to the apostles and through the apostles to a new community called the church.

The Word of God is both disturbing and comforting, judging and saving. It is common to speak of the Word as afflicting the comfortable and comforting the afflicted. At times the distinction is sequential, first one, then the other. At other times, the two actions occur simultaneously, such as the proclamation of the words "The body and blood of Christ—for you." Convicting us of our complicity in the sinfulness of all humanity, that message simultaneously sets us free from the restricting power of sin and death to serve others suffering from sin's systemic invasion of God's world. The form that gospel service takes in the world is social justice.

"You Always Have the Poor with You"

Three of the Gospels report a saying of Jesus that ties together the New Testament and the Hebrew Bible in terms of identity and action. The saying is both bewildering and profound. Unraveling the mystery behind Jesus' words exposes the basis for social justice and human care by the church of Jesus Christ.

Just prior to Jesus' death, a woman anointed Jesus with an expensive ointment. Some observer (or observers) became indignant at her action and wondered why the oil had not been sold and the money given to the poor. Jesus responded to this concern by saying, "You always have the poor with you, but you do not always have me" (Matt. 26:11; Mark 14:7; John 12:8).

How easily we might miss the meaning of the saying by losing ourselves in the narrative's details.[1] Mark, the earliest Gospel, continues Jesus' statement about the constant presence of the poor with the words "and you can show kindness to them whenever you wish" (v. 7). Both Matthew and John eliminated that part of the saying. In Matthew and Mark, Jesus commended the woman and promised that people throughout the world will hold her in remembrance whenever the gospel is preached.[2]

What does Jesus' saying mean? Why would Jesus make a statement that appears to justify extravagance at the expense of the poor? Did Jesus suffer a momentary lapse in the face of his imminent execution? Did he avoid the expressed indignation by merely acknowledging the continuing condition of poverty?

The Poor in the Bible

While the identities of God and Jesus are paramount in the Bible, to understand the foundation for social justice we need also to define "the poor" in the cultural context of the day. Such a pursuit involves several approaches to the word itself. The first step is using a concordance to determine the definitions of the Hebrew and Greek words translated as "poor." Second, noting other words that appear in the same context along with "poor" provides clues for understanding. Sometimes these words will be synonyms; at other times, antonyms will reveal the intended meaning.

Ptochos, the word that Jesus uses in the saying quoted above, is by far the most common word in the New Testament for "poor." In the ancient Greek world, the word pointed to economic destitution and by extension to the social degradation of begging, depending on others for help. Living within the Greek culture, the Jewish community in Alexandria began translating the Hebrew Scriptures into Greek about the middle of the third century BCE. The translators used that common Greek word for a variety of Hebrew words. In their basic meanings, the Hebrew words focus on relational and social degradation even more than economic deprivation. Words like "afflicted," "oppressed," "humbled," "dependent," and "dispossessed" describe the conditions included in "poor."[3]

The New Testament and the writings of the first-century historian Josephus include among the poor both those who work and those who beg. Among those who worked but barely eked out a living were many priests, scribes, rabbis, day laborers, and the *am haaretz* (the Jewish "people of the land" who worked their own land or someone else's). Others, unable to work because of afflictions, depended on begging for their survival. There were also the widows and orphans, who were particularly vulnerable and often barely survived.[4]

Luke's account of the beginning of Jesus' ministry focuses on an excerpt from Isaiah 61 that he read in his hometown synagogue. In that ancient prophecy, the poor appear first in a list that includes the imprisoned, the blind, and the debt-ridden (Luke 4:18). When Luke reports the occasion of a Pharisee's guest list and seating arrangement at a wedding banquet (Luke 14:1-14), Jesus takes the opportunity to suggest that the next party include "the poor, the crippled, the lame, and the blind" (see also the lists at Matt. 11:4-5; 25:34-36; Rev. 3:17). This group of persons existed on the edge of ancient society. They were outcasts. Others considered them cursed and did not allow them in certain sections of the Temple in Jerusalem or in some religious communities, like Qumran.[5]

Another verbal clue for defining the poor lies in the structure of Hebrew poetry. The major characteristic of poetry in the Hebrew Bible is parallelism: two or three lines of poetry relate to one another to provide meaning that is more comprehensive or to extend a thought. Most common is synonymous parallelism, in which a second line repeats the meaning of the first line by using synonyms. Words like "the poor," "the needy," "the weak," "the afflicted" (Job 24:4; Ps. 9:18; 72:4, 12-14; Prov. 14:31; 30:14; 31:20; Amos 2:7), even "hungry," "naked," "oppressed" (Isa. 58:6-7) and "orphan" (Job 29:12) appear as synonyms to one another. Another kind of parallelism uses antonyms; opposite words provide clues for interpretation. One would expect that the opposite of "poor" would be "rich" (the use of the term as in Ps. 49:2 is rare). However, the opposite of "poor" is usually "ruthless," "wicked," "oppressor," "villain," and "godless" (see Job 36:6, 15; Isa. 32:7).

The poor are persons who for various reasons are not able to maintain their honorable status in society or who suffer dishonor at the hands of oppressors.[6] They are not simply persons in economic straits but people suffering such circumstances as debt, homelessness, illness or physical challenges, and the consequences of death. Without using the words for "poor," the scriptures included the widow, the orphan, and the sojourner as persons particularly vulnerable to suffering dishonor (Deut. 24:14, 17; Mark 12:42-43).[7]

The Causes of Poverty

Since "the poor" includes diseased people, persons without homes, children without parents, widows, and victims of crimes and oppression, the causes of such sufferings range among many possibilities in the Bible.[8] Indeed, the reason for human suffering was the subject of some of the oldest literature in the world.

Sometimes, the simple answer was "the Lord makes poor and makes rich" (1 Sam. 2:7) or "the Lord gave, and the Lord has taken away" (Job 1:21). Without stating any motive for God's actions over the fates of people, such passages simply attribute everything that happens to God. In ancient proverbial wisdom there developed a theological explanation for success or failure, wealth or poverty, blessing and curse. God or gods rewarded the wise and righteous with good. Likewise, God punished fools and the wicked with poverty and other sufferings. According to that theology, human laziness was one of the expressions of foolishness that caused poverty (Prov. 6:6-11; 10:5; 19:15). Any disaster required the sufferer to determine what wrong he or she had done and to make amends. This position takes its most eloquent expression in the theology of Job's friends as their response to his suffering.

In the same biblical collections of proverbial wisdom, however, a contrary trend appears. The Lord commands that people should not rob the poor "because they are poor" (Prov. 22:22), without reference to the reason for their poverty. Indeed, one of the realities of life for the poor was that while their hard labor in the fields produced much food, "it is swept away through injustice" (Prov. 13:23). The difference between the haves and the have-nots is not necessarily work or idleness but injustice done to those who have so little to begin with.[9]

On a different and more subtle level, some of the prophets announced unequivocally that God causes some to become poor. The prophets proclaimed that the people of Israel and their leaders dishonored the Lord and defied the Lord's law by their neglect of and failure to care for the poor (Isa. 3:13-15; Jer. 22:13-17; Mic. 2:1-2). God's word of judgment on the oppressors of the poor made the oppressors themselves poor.

When the disciples asked Jesus about the reason a man on the street was blind, they expected the answer to lie in the proverbial response that it was due to sin—the man's or his parents. To their surprise, Jesus removed the man's suffering from the traditional connection with sin and explained that the blindness and resulting life as a beggar was to provide for the miracle that was about to occur: "that God's works might be revealed in him" (John 9:1-2).

Responsibility for the Poor

No matter what reason humans devise to explain why some are poor, God's Word in the Hebrew scriptures stakes divine identity and reputation on their protection and rescue. To serve as God's agents in this divine work, God calls the entire human community and holds especially accountable the covenant people of Israel. Further, God commissioned each Davidic king enthroned in Jerusalem to act as God's agent in administering social justice.

God's identity as defender of the needy is basic to creation and redemption. The wisdom tradition that lies behind Proverbs, Job, Ecclesiastes, and many psalms is universal rather than national, human rather than Israelite, based on creation rather than acts of salvation in a nation's history. "The poor"—whatever their nationality—can look to God as their redeemer and creator.

The Lord's identity as the "redeemer" of orphans serves as a warning against those who would encroach upon their inherited land (Prov. 23:10-11). In ancient Israelite society, the word "redeem" described the action of a close relative who would pay the court costs and other penalties so that an accused person might go free. Familial identity led to action. Further, called "a stronghold for the oppressed" (Ps. 9:9), the Lord serves as defense attorney for the poor and afflicted against their despoilers (Prov. 22:22-23).

The branches of the family tree stretch far in wisdom teaching, because God is the Maker, the Creator of all, rich and poor alike (Prov. 17:5; 22:2). Bestowing kindness to the poor and needy honors God their Maker (Prov. 14:31).

The understanding of God as the Creator of the world, all its life and all its people, became a significant theological development in ancient Israel. Their hymns celebrated their God as Creator and, therefore, as the Ruler of the universe (Pss. 93, 95–99). The Lord rules the world through "justice and righteousness" (Pss. 9:7-8; 96:13; 97:2; 98:9; see also 99:4). The words demonstrate the order by which God rules so that chaos does not prevail. "Justice" describes a harmonious existence for a community as large as humanity or as small as a family. Justice portrays a wholeness and health of life, something like the word *shalom*. "Righteousness" describes specific actions that contribute to a community's justice.[10] Such acts could be the seemingly immoral conduct of Tamar, who seduced her father-in-law to bear a child for the family's survival (Gen. 38), or the activity by which God establishes and maintains justice. The Hebrew word for "righteousness" is sometimes translated "victory" when it speaks of the Lord's acts of deliverance of the world from chaos (Ps. 98:1) or of Israel from bondage (Isa. 52:10).[11] That justice and righteousness are the means by which God rules the world assures the oppressed everywhere that they can trust God to transform their brokenness into wholeness.

The creation account in Genesis 1 declares that God's identity as Creator resulted from the spoken Word. With each dynamic utterance, every part of the cosmos appeared along with its intended function. However we today describe the origins of the universe and of life, the account in Genesis 1 provides meaning for all that exists and especially for the world's humanity. God created humanity "in the image of God. . . . Male and female he created them" (1:27). Two significant teachings result from this one verse. First, God created "them," that is, a community, and all the members of the human community share the same identity. Second, while in other ancient societies the gods created the king in their image—and the people as servants to the king—in this biblical account God bestows the dignity of God's image on the whole human race. No peoples or nations developed until Genesis 10. No distinctions between rich and poor mar the dignity of this universal identity bestowed by God the Creator. Dishonoring the poor "because they are poor" (Prov. 22:22) is a denial of the God-given dignity they share with all the rest of humanity.

Once again, identity and purposeful action intertwine. Royal identity carries with it the royal responsibility (dominion) for the rest of creation. God's Word commissions humanity not to trash (subdue) the earth but to cultivate the land and to nurture all life. The hymn version of this profound narrative appears as Psalm 8.

Out of all the vulnerable in humanity, God chose to reveal a distinct identity to the people who became Israel. Their election was due to God's unmerited love, not to their righteousness (Deut. 9:6) nor to their impressive numbers (Deut. 7:6-8). On "the fewest of all peoples" and "a stubborn people" God staked a reputation that bound together identity and action. Through Moses, God gave the name Yahweh (translated "Lord") for the sole purpose of freeing the oppressed from their bondage in Egypt (Exod. 3:1-15). "I have observed the misery of my people who are in Egypt; I have heard their cry on account of their taskmasters. Indeed, I know their sufferings, and I have come down to deliver them" (Exod. 3:7-8).

The word "cry" is a technical term in Hebrew. It means a plea for help in the face of oppression. Hearing that plea and seeing their plight enabled the Lord to "know" their sufferings. "Knowing" involves not merely awareness but intimate experience. Adam "knew" Eve, and she bore Cain (Gen. 4:1). Out of all the nations on the earth, God "knew" only Israel (Amos 3:2). Painfully involved in the suffering of the Hebrew slaves, the Lord promised to deliver them. Divine identity and action came together in the divine Word.

When the people of Israel would one day again become the poor—as exiles in Babylon—the Lord would hear their cries for help. By that time the people of Israel had even formalized their cries for help into laments, like Psalm 74. Carried off to exile, scoffed at by their enemies, having been made poor, the people cried to God to remember that years ago "you redeemed the tribe of your heritage" (v. 2), that is, the Hebrews in Egypt. Since "redeemed" explained both the relationship of God with the people and the action needed for deliverance, God used it in responding to their lament. "Do not fear, for I have redeemed you," God said through the prophet called Second Isaiah (Isa. 43:1). In case the people missed the implication of the action for God's identity, the prophet introduced the speaker of the next divine speech as "the LORD, your Redeemer, the Holy One of Israel" (v. 14). The same identity introduces a speech in the next chapter. What follows is precisely what distinguishes the Lord from the dumb idols: only the Lord speaks the Word that accomplishes what it promises (Isa. 44:6-8). The good news for the poor and homeless exiles is that the Word of salvation announced by the prophet is already occurring.

In order to accomplish God's work in the world, God employs humans. God assigned responsibility for the poor to humanity as a whole. Since the wisdom literature focused on creation and humanity, its teachings about caring for the poor instruct all people in every nation. The prohibitions against robbing the poor and crushing them in courts of law (Prov. 22:22) are addressed to all persons, not to Israel alone. The judgment of God would fall on all "mortals" whose wickedness caused the cries of the poor and afflicted to reach to heaven (Job 34:21-30).[12]

Specifically, the Lord calls the people of Israel to social responsibility as a major component of the covenant made with them through Moses. God's Word took the form of law to instruct the people about their covenant role. The primary code of behavior for the people the Lord redeemed from Egypt is, of course, the Decalogue (Exod. 20:1-17). The identity of the Lord as the one who brought the people of Israel out of their bondage serves as the basis for the commandments.[13] The Decalogue moves from ways of honoring God to ways of living with one another in society. While family life serves as the basic interhuman relationship, the laws protecting the "neighbor" prohibit all the actions that dishonor persons and make them poor.

Divine commands about caring for the poor appear in considerable detail in other codes of law. Without separating divine law from civil law in this theocracy of biblical Israel, God's Word for social justice is unambiguous in legal collections like the Book of the Covenant (Exod. 21:1—23:22), the Priestly Code (Lev. 19–26), and the Code of Deuteronomy (Deut. 12–26). Contrary to popular opinion, these codes demonstrate the dynamic quality of the laws God gave to Israel. The Book of the Covenant seems to have its origin during the period of the judges (1200–1000 BCE), when the people lived in an agricultural society. The Code of Deuteronomy updated that earlier code five to seven centuries later, when monarchies and urbanization occurred. The Holiness Code, compiled probably in the sixth century BCE, is the amalgamation of laws over several centuries that connect the worship life of the people to their responsibilities in society.

The Lord threatens that any oppression against a resident alien, a widow, or an orphan will have dire consequences, especially when the Lord hears their cries for help (Exod. 22:21-24; see also Lev. 19:33-34; Deut. 24:14, 15, 17; 27:19). Any financial gain at the expense of the poor will lead to divine intervention (Exod. 22:25-27; Deut. 23:19-20). Any perversion of justice against the poor will result in divine indictment (Exod. 23:6-8; Lev. 19:15; Deut. 24:17-18).

In these codes, the Lord organizes the people for social justice in ways that provide food for the poor. God forbids harvesting fields, orchards, and vineyards every seventh year (the Sabbath year) so that the poor might eat (Exod. 23:10-11); God orders the people to leave produce every time they harvest any food in their fields (Lev. 19:9-10; Deut. 24:19-22). The Lord also provides a system for forgiving debt every seventh (Sabbath) year so that people do not remain poor (Deut. 15). Further, the Lord commands more comprehensively that "if any of your kin fall into difficulty and become dependent on you, you shall support them (Lev. 25:35-54).

The motives for God's command that the people of Israel protect and care for the poor and needy are several. Most common is their identification with the vulnerable aliens in Egypt whom the Lord redeemed in the time of Moses. God called them "to remember" their slavery and the exodus (Deut. 5:15; 7:18; 8:2; 15:15; 16:3; 24:18, and often). Such remembering was the basis for celebrating the Passover, for keeping the law, and especially for caring for the vulnerable. That historic deliverance made the people of Israel God's servants (Lev. 25:55) to carry out the divine work of caring for the poor. The motive appears more simply as the divine claim "I am the LORD" (Lev. 19:10 and often), but the people did not know the Lord apart from the act of deliverance (Lev. 19:34).

While God held the entire people of Israel, the redeemed, accountable for the poor and the needy, God focused this responsibility on the kings of David's dynasty. In the restructuring of the people from tribal affiliations to national (monarchic) systems, every Davidic king was anointed on coronation day to be the "son of God" (see 2 Sam. 7:14; Ps. 2:7; 45:7). Their command to rule by God's justice and righteousness included the protection of the poor (Ps. 74:1-4). Such responsibility for royalty was common in the ancient world. Hammurabi, king of Babylon in the eighteenth century BCE, indicated in the prologue to his famous law code that the god Anu appointed him "to cause justice to prevail in the land . . . that the strong might not oppress the weak."[14] Yet sitting on Jerusalem's throne as God's adopted and anointed son (messiah) was different. God was different. Anu lived up to his name (Sky) by remaining aloof in the heavens. While the Lord of Israel likewise lived in heaven (e.g., Deut. 26:15; 1 Kings 8:30, 31, 32), God "came down" to respond to the poor's cries for help, most especially to deliver the poor aliens in Egypt (Exod. 3:8). God's son (each Davidic king) bore this divine commitment to deliver "the needy when they call" (cry for help; Ps. 72:12-14). The king's failure to fulfill that responsibility would lead to God's Word of judgment on the nation (Jer. 22:3-5; 34:1-5).

God's Promises to the Poor

In addition to the promise to hear and respond to the poor's pleas for help here and now, God promised them hope in the future. In contrast to the despair of the moment, "the needy shall not always be forgotten, nor the hope of the poor perish forever" (Ps. 9:18).

As God the Creator had the first word on ordering the world and establishing human community, so God will have the last word: the announcement about the reign of God to come. The prophets envisioned the future reign of God to occur "on the day of the Lord." That day will transform fortunes and fates. God will change bad news to good, especially for the poor. Nations everywhere will learn the Word of God and will recycle war instruments into agricultural tools for the betterment of all nations (Isa. 2:2-4; Mic. 4:1-3). Excluded in the present society by economic and ritual customs, the outcasts and the physically afflicted will become the "in" group when God reigns from Mount Zion, the site of the Temple (Mic. 4:6-7). In the new heaven and on the new earth, the poor will no longer live without homes or go hungry or watch their children die; neither will they labor in vain (Isa. 65:17-25). An anonymous prophet reports that the Lord anointed him "to bring good news to the oppressed" at the time "of the Lord's favor"; the list includes the brokenhearted, the captives and prisoners, and the mourners (Isa. 61:1-3). The people who "will inherit the land" when God conquers the wicked are "those who wait for the Lord," "those blessed by the Lord," "the righteous," and "the meek." As "the poor" these people are the ones whom "the Lord helps . . . and rescues . . . from the wicked" because "they take refuge in him" (Ps. 37).

Clearly, many of the promises of the future kingdom are visions that promise the opposite of what the poor were experiencing in the present. Acknowledging that the Lord has been "a refuge to the poor, a refuge to the needy in distress" (Isa. 25:4), the compiler of the Book of Isaiah announces that "on this mountain" God will invite "all peoples" to a luscious feast and during the party destroy death itself (Isa. 25:6-8). To whom would that promise for the New Day mean more than those who were hungry and grieving?

According to a few prophetic visions, God will establish the coming reign of God and then set over it a king of Davidic descent (Isa. 9:2-7; 11:1-10; Jer. 23:5-6; 33:14-16; Mic. 5:2-4; Zech. 9:9-10). Contrary to past kings' failures, this future Davidic king will indeed rule with God's justice and righteousness. The people who have been living in darkness will be awash in light (Isa. 9:2). Portrayed as a warrior conquering oppressors (Isa. 9:4) and slaying the ruthless and the wicked (the opposites of the poor; Isa. 11:4), he will bear the throne names of Wonderful Counselor, Mighty God, Everlasting Father, and Prince of Peace (Isa. 9:4-6). He will reverse the way "the poor" and "the meek" have been treated in the justice system (Isa. 11:4) and will rule with the wisdom that Solomon requested years earlier for governing the people (1 Kings 3:9-28; Isa. 11:2-3; Jer. 23:5). Like a shepherd, he will feed the people and give them security (Mic. 5:4). Like Solomon (1 Kings 1:44), he will ride on a mule to his coronation in Jerusalem, triumphant, victorious, but humble (Zech. 9:9). God's word about the coming of an ideal Davidic king was itself a blessing for the poor.

Jesus of Nazareth

Along came Jesus. On a completely human level, Jesus qualified as one of the poor. Poverty might have been his choice of lifestyle. According to Mark 6:3, the people called Jesus "the carpenter." In the parallel passage in

Matt. 13:55 the carpenter in the family was Jesus' father, Joseph. In either case, Jesus either had the training for an occupation or actually pursued the occupation for a time. He had the possibility of making an income as an artisan and of lifting himself above the poverty line. In the years of Jesus' ministry, however, the records portray Jesus as an itinerant teacher and preacher with "nowhere to lay his head" (Matt. 8:29). Even if he were a rabbi, as some claimed him to be, he would still need to support himself by another occupation, by picking figs or grain along the roadside or by enjoying the generosity of others.

We have no record of Jesus begging, but other people provided many of his meals. While sometimes a dinner guest in the homes of the well-to-do, Jesus often dined among lepers, tax collectors, and sinners—outcasts by their disease or their occupations (or their lack of one). His life ended between two thieves, condemned—as they also were—by people in religious and political power. From the cross, he quoted several individual psalms of lament, as any pious oppressed person would under such circumstances. His disciples buried him in a borrowed tomb. Jesus' life reported in the Gospels was that of the poor.

Whatever the circumstances of Jesus' livelihood, the people considered him to be (1) a teacher and (2) a miracle-working and judgment-preaching prophet. In those roles, Jesus showed compassion and concern for all people, but especially for the poor.

As a teacher, Jesus used the poor and other excluded persons as role models and instructed others to act on their behalf. After teaching in the Temple one day on a variety of topics, Jesus sat down in a spot from which he observed many people put money in the Temple treasury. He noticed that many rich people put in large sums. What caught his eye and provided an example to follow, however, was "a poor widow" who put in a penny's worth. Without denouncing the rich and their offerings, Jesus praised the poor widow for giving out of her poverty, "all she had to live on" (Mark 12:41-44; Luke 21:1-4).

In a parable about praying diligently and hopefully, Jesus made a role model out of a widow who pleaded persistently to a stern judge. Simply to prevent her from wearing him out, the judge granted her the justice she sought against an opponent in a court case. Likewise, Jesus taught, consistent with God's response to cries for help in the Hebrew Bible, God will grant justice to those who cry out for help day and night (Luke 18:1-8).

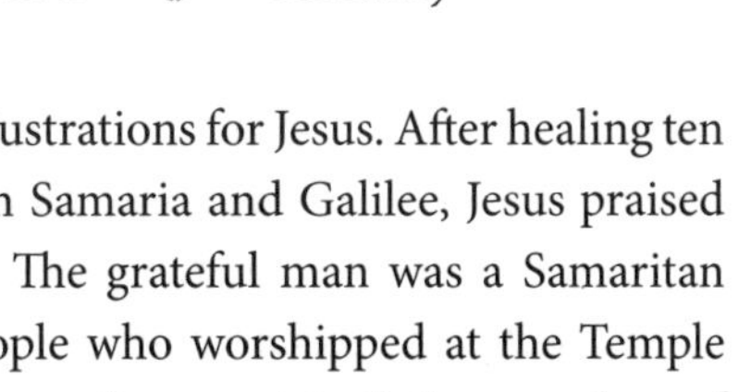

Outcasts also provided teaching illustrations for Jesus. After healing ten lepers in a village somewhere between Samaria and Galilee, Jesus praised the one who returned to thank him. The grateful man was a Samaritan (Luke 17:11-19). For centuries, the people who worshipped at the Temple in Jerusalem despised Samaritans because they went to their own place of worship on Mount Gerizim, not far from Shechem. Of course, the hero in Jesus' parable about the man who was beaten and left to die on the road between Jerusalem and Jericho was a caring and generous Samaritan (Luke 10:29-37).

Particularly striking is Jesus' teaching in the three Synoptic Gospels that above all role models are those who have absolutely nothing to give or to brag about. They, of course, are the infants and little children to whom belongs the kingdom of God (Matt. 18:1-4; 19:13-15; Mark 10:14-16; Luke 18:15-17).

As for those who have possessions, however, Jesus taught what a listener would expect from a good rabbi. God expects those who have to share with those who do not. Abraham—with Lazarus at his side—told the deceased rich man about the uselessness of sending someone from the dead to warn his friends and relatives: they already have Moses and the prophets (Luke 16:29). The law and the prophets were the textbooks for Jesus' teaching. One student who apparently failed the course was the rich ruler whose piety was exemplary until Jesus asked him to sell everything he owned and give the money to the poor (Matt. 19:16-22; Mark 10:17-22; Luke 18:18-23). The rich ruler's sorrowful departure from the classroom stimulated the teacher to deliver a lesson on how difficult it is for the rich to enter the kingdom. Shortly thereafter, Jesus had the opportunity to teach that he was not requiring such total divestment for discipleship. It is a matter of cheerful response, as it was for Zacchaeus, the outcast collector of taxes, who gave half of all that he had to the poor (Luke 19:1-10).

Some of Jesus' unwilling students were those who by profession were experts in the law of Moses: the Pharisees. In many ways, the Pharisees were model citizens. Yet Jesus himself broke all the rules of etiquette for dinner guests by accusing his Pharisee host of greed and wickedness and of neglecting "justice and the love of God" (Luke 11:37-44). Another Pharisee became the antihero of Jesus' parable about self-righteousness and contempt for others. Praying at the Temple, the Pharisee thanked God that he righteously (and admirably) tithed his income. Living up to that rule, he claimed superiority over thieves, rogues, adulterers, and the tax collector beside him. With no admiration for such Pharisaic attitudes, Jesus praised the outcast tax collector for his humility in prayer (Luke 18:9-14). Ironically, the Pharisee's degradation of the tax collector appears in the chapter immediately prior to the story of Zacchaeus, who contributed five times as much.

On the positive side, Jesus taught his followers to "sell your possessions and give alms" (Luke 12:32-34) and to strive to become servants according to his own model (Matt. 20:20-28; 21:11; Mark 10:42-45; Luke 22:25-27). When he commissioned the apostles and the seventy to go out in his name, he commanded that they become poor and count on the hospitality of others (Matt. 10:1-42; cf. 16:24-28; 17:14-21; Mark 6:7-13; 8:34-38; Luke 9:1-6; 10:4-7).

Jesus further demonstrated his teaching skills as he led others (a Pharisee lawyer according to Matt. 22:34-40, a scribe in Mark 12:28-34, a lawyer in Luke 10:25-28) to understand the two greatest commandments: love the Lord your God, and love the neighbor. These two commandments recall the Decalogue in its structure of honoring God and the neighbor, for they incorporate all that the ten laws describe as God's will for the life of the redeemed community.

Jesus compared himself on several occasions to a prophet. In response to the sermon he delivered in his hometown synagogue, Jesus anticipated the imminent rejection by his well-known statement "no prophet is accepted in the prophet's hometown" (Luke 4:24; cf. Matt. 13:57). He proceeded to cite God's outreach to needy Gentiles in the feeding of the widow at Zarephath and the healing of the leprous Naaman by Elijah and Elisha (Luke 4:25-27). Jesus explained the necessity of going to Jerusalem based on the city's reputation for killing prophets (Luke 13:33).

Not surprisingly, then, the people who observed or benefited from some of his miracles considered him to be a prophet. From their scriptures the people knew that Elijah had raised from the dead the only son of the widow of Zarephath (1 Kings 17:17-24).[15] When Jesus raised from the dead the only son of a widow at Nain, the people glorified God, saying, "A great prophet has risen among us!" (Luke 7:11-17). Jesus performed the same miracle for the daughter of Jairus, a leader in the synagogue (Luke 8:40-42, 49-56).

Other miracles would have given Jesus prophetic status. When Jesus fed the hungry multitudes with only a few loaves of bread and ended up with a surplus (Matt. 14:13-21; Mark 6:30-44; 8:1-10; Luke 9:10-17), he had performed the same miracle attributed to Elisha. Admittedly, that ancient prophet had twenty loaves of bread for a mere hundred diners, but Elisha had accomplished his feeding miracle "according to the word of the LORD" (2 Kings 4:38-44). Further, in cleansing lepers, Jesus also followed in the footsteps of Elisha (2 Kings 5:1-14, Naaman the Syrian; see Mark 1:40-45; Luke 5:12-16).

Jesus' own identification with the prophets Elijah and Elisha in the Nazareth synagogue specifically cited God's grace reaching out to Gentiles in need, and his ministry included many examples to verify the popular opinion that he was a prophet. He restored to health the demon-possessed daughter of the Canaanite woman (Matt. 15:28). He healed the slave of a Roman centurion (obviously a Gentile; Luke 7:1-10).

Jesus sounded like a prophet in his preaching. His oracles of woe to unrepentant cities (Matt. 11:20-24) sounded much like the sermons of judgment common in the preaching of Isaiah, Jeremiah, and Ezekiel. His rampage in the Temple and predicting its destruction echoed the actions and words of Jeremiah (Jer. 7, 26). His direct confrontation with religious leaders such as priests, scribes, Pharisees, and Sadducees also ranked him beside Jeremiah.

Not surprisingly, then, when Jesus asked his disciples, "Who do the crowds say that I am?" they reported that popular opinion ranged from John the Baptist to Elijah to some other ancient prophet like Jeremiah who had risen from the dead (Matt. 16:13-14; Mark 8:27-28; Luke 9:18-19). All the candidates in the list were prophets.

The possibility that Jesus was Elijah brought hope to the poor and oppressed. They lived with the promise that just before the dawning of the Day of the Lord—the time when God would transform their sufferings into health and well-being—God would send the prophet Elijah to prepare the way. Disciples of John appeared before Jesus one day to ask, "Are you the one who is to come, or are we to wait for another?" As the story moved along, Jesus spoke of John as "he is Elijah to come" (Matt. 11:2-3, 14). Jesus rejected the title for himself because he was not the forerunner of the promised reign of God.

THE FULLNESS OF TIME

In Jesus the new day was already dawning. Prior to his identifying John as Elijah, Jesus answered the question from John's disciples by pointing to what they had been seeing and hearing (Matt. 11:2-6). They indeed became eyewitnesses to the transformations occurring in the lives of the poor. Persons who had been blind, lame, leprous, deaf, and even dead now knew the opposite of their suffering and its consequences. In an astonishing turnaround, the poor are actually hearing good news. Most of the group appears in the list of those such future blessings would occur in the day of the Lord's favor (Isa. 61:1-2). Raising the dead went far beyond the miracles of Elijah. Resurrection of the dead would come for all people only on the Day of the Lord (Dan. 12:1-4). Lepers, isolated from family and friends because of their disease, returned to their communities, where they would again lead honorable lives. The future hope was occurring in Jesus' ministry. That was the report Jesus instructed the messengers to take back to John: the reign of God was occurring!

In the Beatitudes Jesus summed up the good news for the poor to hear. Whether we read the list in Matt. 5:1-12 or the one in Luke 6:20-23, the poor and those who appear in various lists alongside the poor receive blessings. Luke's version announces that the poor receive the kingdom of God, the hungry eat, the crying laugh, and the persecuted leap for joy "in that day." Matthew adds to the list that the meek inherit the earth (Ps. 37), the merciful receive mercy, the pure in heart see God, and the peacemakers become known as God's children. What distinguishes these two "sermons"—actually lists of blessings—from other "blessing" lists (Deut. 28:1-6; Ps. 84:4-5) and from prophetic promises about the kingdom to come is the unsurpassed good news that in Jesus the day has already begun. Speaking God's Word with divine authority, Jesus is transforming the present into the future and vice versa.[16]

Appropriately, the three Synoptic Gospels begin their stories of Jesus' ministry with Jesus himself announcing the imminence of the promised reign of God. Mark reports that Jesus' first sermon (or indeed the summary of his preaching) announced, "The time is fulfilled, and the kingdom of God has come near; repent, and believe in the good news" (Mark 1:15). Matthew offers an abbreviated form: "Repent, for the kingdom of heaven has come near" (Matt. 4:17). Luke reports Jesus' one-sentence sermon on the text of Isaiah 61: "Today this scripture has been fulfilled in your hearing" (Luke

4:21). The promised kingdom offered wondrously good news for the poor. God's delivering that promise through Jesus, indeed one of them, restored the honor of which oppressors and circumstances had deprived them.

Son of God

Only God could establish the kingdom. Even the prophecies about a future Davidic ruler assumed that God would establish the kingdom before turning it over to the Davidic king, the messiah, to rule. For Jesus to be the instrument of establishing the kingdom, he had to be God or God's Son in a unique way. Mark opens his Gospel, the earliest one, with the words "The beginning of the good news of Jesus Christ, the Son of God" (1:1). That title becomes the theme that ripples throughout the Gospel, beginning with Jesus' baptism and ending in his crucifixion (Mark 1:11; 3:11; 9:7; 15:39).

Among these opportunities to name Jesus as God's Son appear stories that demonstrate he deserves the title. Jesus rebuked the storm and the sea (Matt. 8:23-27; Mark 4:35-41; Luke 8:22-25), an action that only God performed in the Hebrew Bible (Ps. 18:15; Nah. 1:4). The disciples saw Jesus "walking on the sea" (Matt. 14:25-26; Mark 6:48; John 6:19), just as God did at the time of creation to bring order out of chaos (Job 9:8).

The title "Son of God" and the conquering of the sea were parts of the cherished traditions about the Davidic king, the messiah. God adopted as son each king of Davidic descent on the day of his coronation (Ps. 2:7). In a hymn celebrating that divinely bestowed identity and relationship (Ps. 89), the people sang that (1) God's exalted role over all other gods was the result of defeating and stilling the sea (vv. 9–10) and (2) God extended that power to David, the anointed one, the son of God (vv. 25–27).

The Gospels assign both David's title and his power over chaos to Jesus. Was it enough to establish Jesus' identity and purpose? Was the Davidic connection the best foundation for his defending the poor and responding to their cries for help (Ps. 72:1-2, 12-14)? How did Jesus feel about the messianic title?

Only rarely did Jesus accept the title Christ/Messiah for himself. When Jesus asked the disciples about who they thought he was, Peter confessed, "You are the Messiah." Jesus ordered him to keep that confession to himself and immediately began to speak of himself as the Son of Man who must suffer many things and be killed, then rise again (Mark 8:29-31; Luke 9:20-22). In Matthew's version of the same confession, Jesus affirms Peter's confession as deriving from "my Father in heaven" and promises Peter the keys to the kingdom (Matt. 16:16-20). That unqualified acceptance of the title was rare for Jesus. Normally he spoke of himself as Son of Man, a title that identified him as humble, poor, and suffering.

On one occasion, Jesus asked the Pharisees about whose son was the Messiah. They answered exactly as we would expect: "The son of David." But using Psalm 110 to his advantage, Jesus demonstrated that the Messiah is Lord even over Davidic kings (Matt. 22:41-46; Mark 12:35-37; Luke 20:41-44). The customary understanding of the Messiah's identity and origin would not suffice.

If Jesus were the Messiah, the definitions would have to change. His origin could not be established by an adoption formula on coronation day. It would result from his conception (Matt. 1:18-25; Luke 1:26-38) or from "the beginning" of creation (John 1:1). His life would not involve wearing royal purple but serving the poor as one of the poor. He refused to become an earthly king when some, impressed by his feeding miracle, tried to crown him (John 6:15). His victory was not the expected Messiah's conquest on bloody battlefields of opposing armies but one of defeating sin and death and all their chaotic power. His kingdom was much bigger than a mere nation, and the only means of attaining reign over the universe was to defy temptation (Matt. 4:1-11; Luke 4:1-13) and to die as the crucified Messiah.

Without recognizing the Risen Lord walking beside him on the Emmaus road, Cleopas said to Jesus about the crucified prophet in Jerusalem, "We had hoped he was the one to redeem Israel" (Luke 24:21). Clearly, he has not. What a stunning shock to the system that he did not fit the expectations! What a blessing for the poor of the world that he did not! Instead, he is the Crucified and Risen Lord who redeems the whole world from its sin.

This Risen Lord, as Son of Man, will come again in glory (Matt. 25:31-46). Seated on the throne of glory with all the nations before him, the Son of Man will separate the sheep from the goats based on one criterion: how they cared for him in his need. Jesus described his needs as hunger, thirst, isolation, nakedness, illness, and imprisonment. They are some of the conditions that define the poor. In response to the questions about his having these needs, Jesus identified himself with those who have the same needs:

"the least of these who are members of my family." To them, the poor, Jesus said, "Come, you that are blessed by my Father, inherit the kingdom prepared for you from the foundation of the world." He was repeating in his time of glory the same blessing he announced to them on the mountain at the beginning of his humble ministry among them (Matt. 5:3). Jesus' identity as the Suffering, Crucified, and Risen Lord ensured that his word of action was true.

Revisiting "The Poor You Always Have with You"

It appears unlikely that Jesus, one of the poor himself, would simply allude to the ongoing condition of poverty while personally experiencing the woman's display of extravagance. More improbable is that a wise teacher or a prophet would allow such a comment to slip out inadvertently and to be recorded for millennia of readers "wherever the gospel is preached in the whole world." Impossible is the explanation that this newly defined Messiah and Son of God would have resorted to even a moment of royal splendor at the expense of the poor.

Perhaps the clue to what Jesus meant lies in his skill as a teacher. A teacher need only speak the words, "A stitch in time . . . ," and most hearers will be able to finish the sentence and thus relearn the intended lesson. This teaching device has a long history. In the Epistle of Second Peter, the author writes to warn readers about lapsing into disbelief or paganism after having become Christians. One way he teaches this point is by using a most unappetizing image. "It has happened to them according to the true proverb, 'The dog turns back to its own vomit'" (2 Pet. 2:22). The author trusted the readers to finish the sentence—those who were acquainted with the Book of Proverbs would know how. "Like a dog that returns to its vomit is a fool that reverts to his folly" (Prov. 26:11).

When Jesus said, "The poor you always have with you, but you do not always have me," it is possible he was using such a teaching device to convey a lesson that went beyond the spoken words themselves. What would come into the minds of first-century Jews when they heard the words "the poor you always have with you"? Knowing their scriptures, they surely would have recalled the words of the Lord at Deut. 15:11: "Since there will never cease to be some in need on the earth, I therefore command you, 'Open your hand to the poor and needy neighbor in your land.'"

The quotation is part of the instructions for the Sabbath year, when the people of Israel were required to forgive all debts. The people of Israel were "blessed" in the land, and so there will be "no one in need among you" (15:4). God commanded the well-to-do to "give liberally and be ungrudging when you do so" (15:10). God expected an open hand simply because, contrary to God's will, there were some poor and needy people.

By alluding to this entire verse and the context in which it stands, Jesus would have been alerting his listeners to remember God's command to reach out to the poor, even as he simultaneously allowed the woman to honor him by anointing his body for burial a few days later. Such is the lesson we would expect from Jesus, God's Son, in light of his impending crucifixion.

The anointing by the woman preceded an unrepeatable act, the burial of his crucified body. Only a few verses later, according to Matthew and Mark, Jesus instituted the Lord's Supper by which the Twelve and their generations of successors would partake of the meal in the presence of the Crucified Messiah (Matt. 26:26-29; Mark 14:22-25). While the anointing for burial is not repeatable, Jesus instituted the meal precisely for repeatability.

According to Paul's record of Jesus' words of institution, after the sayings about the bread and about the cup, Jesus added, "Do this . . . in remembrance of me" (1 Cor. 11:25). Whether or not the Last Supper was originally a Passover meal, Jesus' words effectively replaced the Passover-exodus event as the motive for the meal and for care of the poor and the needy. The people of Israel "remembered" the exodus in the Passover and identified with the redeemed of that historical event as the motive for the humanitarian laws. Now, Jesus calls the church to remember him by the meal based on his crucifixion, identify with those around the table, and anticipate the banquet in the kingdom to come. In the process, the Word of God brings the Crucified Lord into our midst, nourishes us poor beggars who come to the table with nothing to offer (as Luther said), refreshes us needy ones with amazing grace, and creates anew a community called by the Spirit.

In the chapter following his recording of the anointing scene, the author of John's Gospel reports Jesus' new commandment: "Love one another as I have loved you." Jesus based this commandment to love solely on his own sacrificial love for us. (The tense of the Greek verb behind "as I have loved you" points to a specific act rather than to continuing fondness.) The church's motive to love personally and publicly (socially) is based not on the exodus, but on the sacrifice of Christ.

The Church of the Crucified and Risen Lord

The existence of the church provides both the evidence that the promised reign of God began in Jesus and the realization that God's universal reign is still to come. The church is the community of the end-time, although the end is not yet here. Jesus performed miracles as signs of the dawning of the kingdom, but night exists simultaneously. People still get sick and die, people still wrong one another, and people still hunger and weep. Between the time of Jesus and his coming again, the church is "the meantime." God creates the church by the Word, sustains the church by the Word, and entrusts the church with the Word. The church's identity is the Body of Christ in the world here and now. The church's work is God's incarnational involvement in the world's sufferings.

As the author of Luke-Acts continues the story of Jesus and the church in the Book of Acts, he describes the early church as a sharing community.[17] God formed the community on Pentecost, fulfilling the prophecy from Joel 2:28-29 that promised the outpouring of the Spirit on men and women, old and young, male and female slaves. The comprehensive list of the Spirit's recipients created a new community that would become "the church." The early church expressed its oneness as a community of the Spirit by sharing with one another. When needs arose among the members, others would sell some of their property to provide. They ate meals together and praised God together. Their lifestyle attracted new members (see Luke 2:43-47). As a result of their caring for one another, "there was not a needy person among them" (4:34; recall Deut. 15:4-11). Of course, no community is perfect, and while Joseph Barnabas was exemplary for his generosity, Ananias and Sapphira lied about theirs (Acts 4:36—5:11).

A tension over the distribution of goods actually led the early church to organize itself for social justice. The Hellenists in the congregation complained that the church was favoring Hebrew widows over Greek widows. The challenge led to a community meeting, which resulted in the appointment of seven men to organize and distribute food among the members. By their names, the chosen seven were Greeks (Acts 6:1-6). The development of an organized delivery system of care seemed to impress others to join the community (6:7).

The early community provided us with our first example of the church's response to disaster (Acts 11:27-30). A Christian prophet named Agabus went to Antioch and predicted a worldwide famine. Apparently, Jerusalem was hit especially hard, and the Christian community there was in great need. The disciples in Antioch gave what they could for those in Jerusalem and commissioned Barnabas and Saul (Paul) to deliver the financial support.

The author of Luke-Acts reports Paul's moving farewell speech to the elders at Ephesus (Acts 20:17-35). Paul summarizes his work among them, particularly his fidelity to preaching the gospel of Christ and the kingdom of God. As he concludes his speech, the apostle reminds them that he supported himself with his own labor, an example for them that "we must support the weak, remembering the words of the Lord Jesus, for he himself said, 'It is more blessed to give than to receive.'" While we have no other evidence of these words from Jesus, they are words we would expect from the Crucified Christ.

The Epistle of James, though not really an epistle but a homily, earned Luther's definition as "an epistle of straw," because the author spent little time proclaiming the gospel. More like a teacher than a preacher, the author demands that members of the Christian community treat one another without partiality. Although the author is one of the few in the Bible who sets poor and rich as opposites (1:9-11), he demands that the congregation treat equally those who are rich and those who are poor (2:1-4). The people seem to have forgotten that God chose "the poor in the world to be rich in faith and to be heirs of the kingdom" (2:5-6). In the tradition of the Hebrew Bible law, prophets, and writings, he defines as the purest religious responsibility "to care for orphans and widows in their distress, and to keep oneself unstained by the world" (1:27).

The letters of the apostle Paul are the earliest works in the New Testament. Instead of a chronological presentation of social justice in the New Testament, the first becomes last in the present discussion—because Paul took the question to a different level. Writing and preaching in the middle of the first century, Paul left unmentioned Jesus' birth, baptism, and healing miracles—all so prominent in the Gospels. Paul focused in sermons and letters almost exclusively on the announcement and meaning of Jesus' death, resurrection, and ascension (see his sermon in Antioch at Acts 13:16-41).

Paul's most systematic presentation of his theology is, of course, his Epistle to the Romans. The structure of the epistle moves from God's justification of sinners to the service forgiven sinners render to one another. At the outset, Paul focuses on identity. He identifies himself as "a servant of Jesus Christ" and defines Jesus as Son—humanly a descendant of David but declared to be the Son of God based on his resurrection from the dead (1:1-4). Paul develops his letter in three major sections: (1) All humanity is guilty of sin—Gentiles on the basis of idolatry and Jews by their disobedience to the law (1:18—3:20). (2) "So that he might be merciful to all" (11:32), "the righteousness of God[18] through faith in Jesus Christ" justifies (that is, acquits) the guilty (3:21-26; recall the meaning of "righteousness" in the Hebrew Bible as a saving action that results in victory). Paul proclaims the meaning of God's justification through the end of chapter 11. (3) God's saving action calls for a response of incarnational and sacrificial service to the world (12:1—16:27). Ernst Käsemann wrote about this section: "Christian freedom and the new obedience manifest themselves only as the message of the gospel that God has reached out to the world and wills to have this confirmed and symbolically represented by the earthly conduct of the community."[19] This incarnational response by the justified means, among other things, recognizing that the whole will of God is summed up in the commandment "Love your neighbor as yourself" (13:9), an assertion Paul had already written to another congregation (Gal. 5:14). Such love demands that Christians treat one another with the hospitality that Christ showed for us (Rom. 14:1; 15:7).

In this and other letters, Paul used the word "liturgy" for the church's response in the world. Staying true to the use of the word in classical Greek and Roman societies,[20] Paul spoke of financial contributions as liturgical acts. He considered the sharing of resources by the people in Macedonia and Achaia with "the poor among the saints at Jerusalem" to be their *leitourgia*, translated "service" (Rom. 15:26-27). In another letter, too, he commended the churches in Macedonia: "during a severe ordeal of affliction, their abundant joy and their extreme poverty have overflowed with a wealth of generosity on their part" (2 Cor. 8:2). Paul used their example to remind the Corinthians of their promise to send money for the poor Christians in Jerusalem. The contribution from their congregations (consisting of the foolish, the weak, the low, and the despised, according to 1 Cor. 1:26-31) would be their *leitourgia*, translated "ministry" (2 Cor. 9:12). Such a liturgy of financial support "not only supplies the needs of the saints but overflows with many thanksgivings to God." (Notice how the two great commandments about loving God and the neighbor come together here.) In another letter, Paul uses the same word for "liturgy" as he thanks the Philippians for sending Epaphroditus to minister to him in his imprisonment (Phil. 2:25, 30). The "liturgist" here is the one sent and supported by a community of faith to minister to a person in need.

A significant point in Paul's argument to raise contributions for the poor from the Corinthian Christians was the example of Christ. "For you know the generous act of our Lord Jesus Christ, that though he was rich, yet for your sakes he became poor, so that by his poverty you might become rich" (2 Cor. 8:9). It is tempting to consider that Paul was referring to the lifestyle of Jesus discussed above. However, since the apostle wrote so little about Jesus' life and ministry, he is more likely thinking of the hymn he quoted elsewhere about the humbling and exalting of Christ Jesus:

> who, though he was in the form of God . . .
> . . . emptied himself,
> taking the form of a slave,
> being born in human likeness. (Phil. 2:6-7)

In this humbling incarnation of the Son of God, in his subsequent death on a cross, and in his exaltation lies the most powerful motive for the church to honor and care for the poor and needy.

INVITATION TO SOCIAL MINISTRY

The Bible witnesses to the Word of God that judges and saves its listeners. God's Word changes our identity and summons us to be whose we have become. While present-day theories of evolution demonstrate the principle of "the survival of the fittest," God calls people of faith to serve the weakest. The call is fitting for the God who came down repeatedly to respond to the cries of the oppressed and ultimately "became flesh and lived among us" (John 1:14), suffered and died for our sins, was raised to new life, and through it all became our Crucified and Risen Lord.

The scriptures invite us to recall the social ministry of Jesus in the context of his Hebrew Bible, to hear his teachings about restoring dignity to the oppressed, and to imitate his hospitality to those who know only hostility in the world. Above all, however, "wherever the good news is proclaimed in the whole world," the gospel calls us to finish the sentence: "You will always have the poor with you." Just as the woman in the story honored Jesus two thousand years ago, so through words and actions of liturgy in the world, the church honors the Crucified and Resurrected Lord until he comes again.

For Further Reading

Gerstenberger, Erhard S., and Wolfgang Schrage. *Suffering*. Trans. John E. Steely. Nashville: Abingdon, 1980.

Kysar, Robert. *Called to Care: Biblical Images for Social Ministry*. Minneapolis: Fortress Press, 1991.

McCurley, Foster R. *Go in Peace, Serve the Lord: The Social Ministry of the Church*. Chicago: ELCA Division for Church in Society, 2000.

Pilgrim, Walter. *Good News to the Poor: Wealth and Poverty in Luke-Acts*. Minneapolis: Augsburg Publishing House, 1981.

Reumann, John. *Righteousness in the New Testament*. Philadelphia: Fortress Press, 1982.

Robbins, Jerry K. *Carevision: The Why and How of Christian Caregiving*. Valley Forge, Pa.: Judson, 1993.

2

The Relief of the Needy in Their Distress

Early and Medieval Christian Social Initiatives

Samuel Torvend

During the reign of the Roman emperor Claudius (41–54 CE), significant portions of the eastern Mediterranean suffered a severe and crippling famine that caused widespread starvation, prompted the dislocation of impoverished peasants, and nurtured uprisings among a people who suffered foreign occupation. The Jewish historian Josephus reports that in the midst of this crisis, Queen Helen of Adiabene—a recent convert to Judaism eager to demonstrate her concern for the Jewish population of the province—purchased grain shipments for the relief of the languishing population in Jerusalem.[1]

The disastrous effects of the famine were also noted in the earliest letters of Paul of Tarsus, a recent convert to the Jesus movement and a Christian missionary in the urban centers of the Mediterranean. He wrote to the Corinthians: "Now concerning the collection for the saints [in Jerusalem]: you should follow the directions I gave to the churches of Galatia. On the first day of the week, each of you is to put aside and save whatever extra you earn, so that collections need not be taken when I come. And when I arrive, I will send any whom you approve with letters to take your gift to Jerusalem" (1 Cor. 16:1-3; see Gal. 2:10; 2 Cor. 8:1—9:15; Rom. 15:25-27; Acts 11:29-30). In his instruction, Paul notes that on the first day of the week—Sunday, the day of resurrection and the emerging day of Christian worship—the Christian assembly is to gather a collection for others who are in need. In his second letter to the Christians at Corinth, he speaks of the privilege of "sharing" in this ministry to the saints (2 Cor. 8:1-4). While the term "sharing" certainly designated a collection of funds for the poor, it also signified participation in the Lord's Supper, an equitable sharing of food and drink by the gathered assembly (see 1 Cor. 10:16). Thus, the *koinonia* of the supper could be extended into a sharing of funds with the hungry poor in Jerusalem. Indeed, this collection from the many house churches is one of the earliest witnesses to Christian initiatives among those who experienced economic and social distress. It was a social practice, nonetheless, rooted in a theology of the generous self-giving of Jesus, the central figure in the Christian story, and his sharing food with the hungry poor (see Matt. 14:13-21; Mark 6:30-44; Luke 9:10-17; John 6:1-13).

Such concern for the victims of famine was rooted in and shaped by the "generous act of our Lord Jesus Christ, that though he was rich, yet for your sakes he became poor, so that by his poverty you might become rich" (2 Cor. 8:9). Christian response to the hungry poor, Paul suggests, flows from the life of Christ "who, though he was in the form of God, did not regard equality with God as something to be exploited, but emptied himself, taking the form of a slave, being born in human likeness" (Phil. 2:6-7). While the liturgical hymn that Paul quotes in his letter to the Christian assembly at Philippi would exert considerable influence in the historical development of a "servant" Christology, its premise—the form of God revealed in human form as slave or servant—may have proved odd or laughable to many in the ancient world.

To anyone raised in a Judeo-Christian or Islamic culture, the pagan gods seem almost trivial. Each is but one of a host of gods and godlings of very limited scope, power, and concern. Moreover, they seem quite morally deficient. They do terrible things to one another, and sometimes they play ugly pranks on humans. But, for the most part, they appear to pay little attention to things "down below." The simple phrase "For God so loved the world . . ." would have puzzled an educated pagan. And the notion that the gods care how humans treat one another would have been dismissed as patently absurd.[2]

In the ancient Mediterranean context in which Christianity emerged, it was well-known that the gods demanded or expected offerings from humans as a form of appeasement or inducement for divine favors. To suggest, however, that one who was "in the form of God" emptied himself "taking the form of a slave"—to suggest that political, religious, or social power would appear in the form of a household servant—would have seemed utterly ludicrous. That a god or a god's representative would be deeply marked by mercy for a distressed humanity, especially the most vulnerable, would have only underscored the novelty of this emerging movement named after a criminal executed by the Roman imperial army. "Classical philosophers," notes Rodney Stark, "regarded mercy and pity as pathological emotions—defects of character to be avoided by all rational [people] . . . [a] defect of character unworthy of the wise. . . . [Indeed] Plato had removed the problem of beggars from his ideal state by dumping them over its borders."[3]

Let us be clear: to contrast ancient perceptions of seemingly divine disregard for human need with early Christianity sensibilities is *not* to suggest that the ancient Mediterranean world was devoid of mercy or that Christians alone promoted social commitments to the needy. For Greeks or Romans who possessed the means to do so, *philanthropia* was considered a noble calling that could be practiced throughout a lifetime. Greek philosophers and their Roman successors encouraged the pursuit of private and public virtues. The Stoics promoted the notion that *all* humans—endowed with divine reason—were to be honored with justice regardless of social status. Likewise, the offering of assistance to the needy was not a mere option for Hellenistic Jews who populated the urban centers around the Mediterranean Sea. Rather, a rich and vibrant Jewish ethical sensibility was the very matrix in which Christian social commitments first emerged. After all, Jesus of Nazareth was a Palestinian Jew steeped in the ancient memory of God's provision for a needy and destitute people (Exod. 12:43-49), a powerful memory commemorated each year in the celebration of the Passover meal. What the Pauline collection from Gentiles for Jewish Christians attests to, nonetheless, is a movement of social and ethical concern beyond ethnic identity as well as a criticism of perceived apathy among the gods of Rome and their human representatives.

In the emerging house churches scattered throughout the Roman Empire, Paul envisioned in Christian baptism the washing away of distinctions between Jews and Gentiles (Gal. 3:25-29). He promoted an equitable sharing of food and drink between wealthy and poor at the Lord's Supper and chastised those who failed at such an equitable sharing of God's own food and drink (1 Cor. 11:17-34). In a patriarchal culture, the historical Paul valorized women as benefactors, leaders, and deacons of the church (Rom.

16:1-16).[4] He spoke of this network of communities in the rich metaphor of the *body*—the Body of Christ—united in its common baptism, supper, and public service to the most vulnerable members of every ancient city: the hungry, the thirsty, the stranger, the naked, the sick, the orphan, the widow, and the imprisoned.[5]

While popular North American perceptions of the ancient Roman world have been shaped by idealized and sanitized cinematic interpretations, the reality of urban life in which Christianity emerged was harsh and brutal. Wealthy elites could live in spacious villas on high ground above the malodorous markets, sewers, and tenement dwellings of the poor. They enjoyed the attention of numerous household slaves, ample food, select wines, private bathing facilities, and recourse to physicians. Such was not the case for the vast majority of the population. While contemporary reconstructions of the ancient city focus on the architectural achievement of temple, coliseum, senate, villa, roadway, aqueduct, and palace, most ancient people lived in a world of urban misery. Indeed, the modern favela, ghetto, and shantytown more closely approximate the context in which Christian house churches emerged.

In his detailed study of Roman urban life, Jérôme Carcopino set forth the many elements that produced physical and psychological stress, disease, and violence.[6] Most Romans, for instance, lived in five- or six-story apartment buildings in which a family rented but one room—a room without running water, without sanitary facilities, with no furnace or fireplace and only an open brazier that could easily topple and start a fire. Such an apartment—the place in which many early Christian communities gathered—had open windows that permitted insect infestation and malaria brought by the hungry mosquito. With no soap and no baths for the many, people were rarely clean. By ancient standards, Rome boasted a sophisticated sewer system, yet many if not most apartment dwellers threw their refuse into the open ditches that ran down the middle of the street. The Romans were adept at building aqueducts for water conveyance into the city, but most people had to carry their daily water in jars from a public fountain to their room-apartment. While wealthy elites had access to many foods and forms of food preparation, a daily diet of bread, wine, a root vegetable, and cheap fish sauce was the norm throughout the Mediterranean.

Given the remarkably crowded conditions in which people lived, it was quite easy for disease to spread among a populace knowing nothing of antibiotics. Where people are unclean, surrounded by waste matter, and easy prey for germs and hungry insects, disease springs to life and moves rapidly. Indeed, it can be comforting to imagine the first Christians living in a world that approximates the middle-class status of most North American Christians. Yet in cities marked by infrastructure that favored only the few, the many were born into a life expectancy of no more than thirty years, a guarantee that they would grow up weak, develop a disability, or contract a fatal disease. Such conditions could readily produce a sense of despair or the violent disruptions among people who sense a gross injustice in the world. Is it any wonder that the deep yearning for health and wholeness, for support and hospitality would well up in a social context marked by such misery? And is it any wonder that health—*salvus* in the Latin, salvation—would be a profound symbol shaping Christian commitments in the midst of the city?

The Body of Christ
Caring for the Needs of the Body

To be sure, there is no social program or policy statement in the Christian scriptures. What these writings reveal, in part, are the different cultural contexts in which early Christianities sprang to life and the attempt of these Christian communities to live together in the expansive image of the Body within the body politic of the ancient city. That they were aware of and responded to the poor and vulnerable members of their communities can be traced to the memory of Jesus, now spoken and enacted in the house churches emerging in Syria and Spain, Rome and Jerusalem, Egypt and Asia Minor. As Mark, the earliest Gospel, notes: Jesus was baptized in flowing water (1:9-11), proclaimed the advent of God's beneficent reign (1:14-15), called forth a community (1:16-20), offered free healing to untouchables (1:40-45), shared meals with the disreputable and the poor (2:15-17; 6:30-44); violated sacred law in order to provide food and healing (2:23-28; 3:1-6); announced an equitable sharing of God's gifts (10:17-27); exercised power in the form of service (10:32-45); and denounced those who robbed widows of their meager resources (12:38-44). It would seem, then, that the manner of his living—what Christians believed was the embodiment of the beneficent reign of God—led to his death at the hands of the imperial army, a death that took place at the very time when the powerful memory of God's deliverance and provision of an enslaved and destitute people was celebrated at Passover.

What one finds scattered through the New Testament is attention to real human need—the offering of nourishment and healing—as well as denunciation and violation of law in order to serve that need. While there is no social policy or program in these texts, there is this: the vibrant memory of Jesus' words and actions that would form a community for its public life and service—its *diakonia*—among those who were overlooked, forgotten, or deemed insignificant by the powerful in market, court, or palace. "In the one Spirit we were all baptized into one body," wrote Paul, ". . . and we were all made to drink of one Spirit" (1 Cor. 12:13). That body—the public Body of Christ—was formed by water and the Spirit, guided by words proclaimed, and nourished on food and drink for its engagement with daily life. The memory of Jesus' own baptism, proclamation, healing, and table fellowship flowed into and shaped the life and mission of this "body" in the world.

Within fifty years of Paul's itinerant work to establish or encourage urban households of faith, the Christian movement throughout the empire and beyond it was growing into residential communities guided by leaders charged with supervision of the church's service among the poor and vulnerable. In his letter to the Christians at Rome, Paul had commended "our sister Phoebe, a deacon of the church at Cenchreae . . . a benefactor of many and of myself as well" (Rom. 16:1-2). Some thirty to forty years after Paul wrote his letter to Rome, Luke narrated the selection of the seven who would care for the distribution of food to destitute widows in Jerusalem (Acts 6:1-6). Among them was Stephen, a preacher and table servant of the poor, whom later Christian tradition would identify as the first martyr and deacon in the church of Christ. Only a few decades later, Ignatius, the supervisor or bishop of Antioch, asked the Christians of Asia Minor to "let the deacons be entrusted with the ministry of Jesus Christ," that is, with a public ministry of service intended to illuminate and guide the *diakonia* of the entire Christian assembly (Letter to the Magnesians 6).

Within fifty years of Ignatius's martyrdom in Rome, a former pagan philosopher and Christian convert named Justin wrote his *First Apology*, addressed to the emperor Antoninus Pius (138–161) and his adopted sons, Marcus Aurelius and Lucius Verus. In this explanation of the Christian faith, Justin set forth the manner in which the words and actions of Jesus entered the life of the Christian assembly:

> On the day named after the sun, there is a meeting in one place of those who live in the city or in the countryside. Then the records of the apostles or the writings of the prophets are read for as long as time permits. When the reader has finished, the presider in a discourse urges and invites us into the imitation of these good things. Then we all stand together and offer prayers. And, as we said before, when we have finished the prayer, bread is set out, together with wine and water. The presider offers up prayer and thanksgiving as best he can, and the people sing out their assent saying the *amen*. There is a distribution of the things over which thanks has been said and each one participates, these things are then sent by the deacons to those who are absent. Those who are prosperous and who desire to do so contribute what they wish, as much as each one chooses, and the collection is deposited with the presider. He cares for orphans and widows, those who are in want because of sickness or any other cause, those who are imprisoned and foreigners who are sojourners among us. In short, the presider is the guardian for all those in need.[7]

What one discerns in this second-century text from Rome is the intimate connection between Christian worship (*leitourgia*, liturgy)—with its affinity for Luke's narration of the Emmaus encounter[8]—and Christian service to the poor and vulnerable (*diakonia*, service). Indeed, one can hear the echo of Stephen's service at table among the poor, of Ignatius's insistence that Jesus Christ does not rule over but serves the least of these in the world. Here, in Roman urban culture, the words and actions of Jesus had become a pattern for gathering: for the reading and interpretation of scripture, for the prayers concerning all those in need, for thanksgiving at table over food and drink, for eating and drinking together, and for the subsequent collection of the assembly's gifts to be guarded and distributed by its presider. And all this took place on Sunday, with its promise that diminishment and death would yield to health, wholeness, and life. "Instead of ignoring the poor while religiously eating to the full (1 Cor. 11:21-22), the community, now, at least according to its ideals, receives the ritual part of the meal and gives most of the food away. Now the juxtaposition of word and meal ritual inevitably involves a third focus: the poor."[9]

What one discerns in Justin's description is the breathing out of the Christian assembly into real human need. While a modern Western reader of the *First Apology* might imagine that the state provided homes for orphans, pensions for widows, and "charity" hospitals for the sick poor, such was not the case. Without a male relative upon whom she could rely for housing and food, a widow would become impoverished, homeless, and forced to beg in the streets or sell herself as a prostitute. Whether he were wealthy or poor, a father had absolute legal rights over any of his offspring; he could readily and legally expose a female or deformed male newborn to the elements or throw an infant into the streets. While Greek and Roman physicians offered medical care to those few who could afford it, the many who suffered with chronic sickness, deformity, or mental instability and illness were left to their own devices or to the care and medical illiteracy of a family. What one discerns in this brief description of Christian worship are the very means through which the memory and practice of Jesus was made available to Christians of succeeding generations. What one discerns in the collection Justin describes is both the memory of Jesus' practice and the beginning of a structured form of generosity—of social service—in a culture where the strong truly survived and the weak truly and easily perished.

What becomes apparent in the second and third centuries is the growth of Christian responses to "the least of these" (Matt. 25:40). Jesus' denunciation of those who rob and take advantage of widows was proclaimed in the Christian liturgy and translated into a series of social initiatives that provided assistance to widows. Yet concern for widows could be extended to all women. Early Christians denounced female infanticide and refused to practice it, condemned incest and marital infidelity, encouraged marriage at an older age than the prepubescent norm, relied on women as house church patrons, and, in some parts of the empire, welcomed them as deacons charged with both liturgical and social service. Thus, the oft-heard claim that Christianity was especially attractive to women rests in the evidence that Christian communities actually valued women more than the larger culture in which they lived and in very concrete ways.

Of course, this is not to suggest that female infants, prepubescent girls, married women, and elderly widows enjoyed liberation from socially oppressive convictions and practices that might be deemed odious today.

Rather, it is to claim that some or many women would be attracted to a community that ignored the law by suggesting that a mother did not need to see her newborn daughter murdered before her eyes simply because her husband wanted a son to carry on his name. Widows would be drawn to a community that claimed them as persons of value and dignity, women who did not need to rush to remarry just any male, brute or beau, who would take them in. They might be drawn to a community that claimed their wisdom and experience by enrolling them in an ecclesial order, where they enjoyed the companionship of other women. Thus, it would be inaccurate to imagine that early Christian social initiatives supporting women constituted a "golden age" that went into later decline. It would be appropriate to recognize that even incremental changes could make the difference between life and death for an infant, a girl, or a widow.

Stories of free and mobile healing by Jesus for social outcasts and the poor were read in the Christian liturgy and developed into a rudimentary form of health care in times of critical need. While many early Christians ignored or condemned the medical advances of Greek physicians (because they were pagans) and thought that the occurrence of disease or epidemic in the natural order could be traced to supernatural causes, they did not appear to be frightened of death. In both Christian and Roman sources, one reads again and again of Christian "fearlessness" in the face of death from disease, epidemic, or persecution. In 165, the probable year of Justin's martyrdom under the emperor Marcus Aurelius, a smallpox epidemic swept through the empire, killing 25 to 35 percent of the population. The epidemic lasted close to fifteen years, and its lethal effects did not diminish for some time after. In less than one hundred years after the first pandemic, a second fell upon the empire in 251 and produced exceptionally high mortality rates. At its most severe, the mortality statistics of Rome show the deaths of five thousand people each day in the city.

Dionysius, the bishop of Alexandria, spoke of this epidemic and Christian responses to the plague:

> Pestilence assailed us. [To the pagans] it was more intolerable than any other calamity . . . but to us this was not so. . . . Most of our [Christian people] were unsparing in their love and kindness. They held fast to each other and visited the sick fearlessly, and ministered to them continually, serving them in Christ. And

> they died with them . . . taking the affliction of others, and drawing the sickness from their neighbors to themselves, [knowing that they would] receive their pains. And many who cared for the sick and gave strength to others died themselves having transferred to themselves their death. . . . They then made real in action [their convictions]. Truly many of our people departed life in this manner . . . so that this form of death, through strong faith it exhibited, seemed to lack nothing of martyrdom. And they took the bodies of the saints in their open hands . . . and closed their eyes and their mouths. They bore them away and laid them out . . . and they prepared them suitably with washings and garments. And after a little they received like treatment themselves, for the survivors were continually following those who had gone before them.[10]

In his report of the epidemic and Christian assistance to its victims, Dionysius notes that no one escaped its devastating effects: gender and ethnicity, religious affiliation and social status mattered not. Later in his letter, he would claim that pagans, because they feared death, deserted their dying friends and even threw their own dead "like refuse" into the street for others to bury. In contrast to this negative portrayal of the general population, he emphasizes the willingness of Christians to care for the sick and dying. The motive for such care, however, is worthy of consideration: for Christians, he claims, death was not the end but a continuing passage into the unending life of the risen Christ, a passage begun in Christian baptism.

Such a conviction—the promise of everlasting life for all the baptized—enabled members of the Christian community to offer rudimentary forms of health care to the sick and dying even though such contact could lead to "drawing the sickness from their neighbors to themselves." Thus, simple forms of free health care—companionship for those isolated by illness, cleaning the sick or dying and disposing of their waste, offering them food and drink, giving them clean clothing—would have given the sick an incremental advantage over those who received no assistance whatsoever. While the modern reader might assume that government offices or charitable institutions would respond to a health crisis of great magnitude and mortality—that assumption itself a relatively recent development in human history—such was not the case in the ancient Roman and Western medieval world.

What one can imagine in the convergence of epidemic, insufficient medical knowledge, and the offering of free nursing by a minority community is how such commitments might appear to pagans: both novel and "miraculous." If there is any truth in the claim that elementary forms of health assistance can steady or reduce mortality rates, then Christian willingness to serve the sick and dying, with the clear risk of contagion and death, would have offered a striking contrast to those who never ventured forth to assist others in need or simply fled the epidemic. The Christian community claimed that in Christ there was the promise of life and wholeness beyond death. Such a conviction served as a powerful motivation to undertake risky assistance.

The stories of Jesus offering free healing to those with contagious or horrifying afflictions (Mark 1:40-45; 5:1-13), read and preached in the Christian liturgy, offered the worshipping assembly a trajectory, as it were, from liturgy to service among those who were shunned or forgotten in their own time. Cyprian, the bishop of Carthage in North Africa, understood the epidemic not as a form of supernatural punishment but as a testing of one's integrity: "Pestilence . . . searches out the justice in every one and examines the human race: whether the healthy care for the sick, whether relatives dutifully love their kinfolk as they should, whether masters show compassion for their ailing servants, whether physicians do not desert the afflicted. . . . These are trying exercises for us, not deaths; they bring to mind the glory of fortitude. By contempt of death, they prepare for the crown [of everlasting life]."[11] In the writings of Dionysius and Cyprian we thus find a correlation between nursing in times of affliction and the experience of martyrdom, that is, a public response to his invitation to "care for me when I [am] sick" (Matt. 25:36) and a public witness of one's commitment to Christ, even when that commitment would endanger one's life.

In the Christian worshipping assembly, the stories of Jesus' meal practice were proclaimed, and a meal was shared in his memory. Together, the practice of Jesus, the admonition of Paul, and the practice of Justin's community focused early Christians on those who had limited access to or were deprived of the most basic human needs: food and drink. Without these two, life simply ended. Paul speaks of an early Christian meal practice—the Lord's Supper—in which thanksgiving to God is made over bread, a meal follows in which all partake, and then thanksgiving to God is made over a cup of wine, "the new covenant in my blood" (1 Cor. 11:23-26). In his criticism of the Corinthian Christians, he charges them with ignoring the memory of Jesus' meal practice among the poor and needy: the wealthy have plenty to eat and drink and even begin the meal before the poor arrive, so that little if any food or drink is left. Such factional inequity is "not really . . . the Lord's supper" (1 Cor. 11:20-23) because it denies the equitable sharing of food and drink among the poor as practiced by Jesus.

At the beginning of the second century, the emperor Trajan banned all unauthorized supper clubs (*collegia illicita*) where the possibility of political resistance could be nourished. From the Roman perspective, Christian gatherings with communal meals fell under the ban of illicit "colleges" or gatherings. Among Christians, the communal sharing of a meal dropped out, while the practice of offering thanks over bread and wine in memory of Jesus on the night before his death remained. Thus, what most modern Christians experience in the Eucharist, or Holy Communion, is the beginning and ending of the earlier Christian meal practice, a fragment of the ancient Mediterranean meal as practiced by Jewish and Gentile Christians. But what of the full supper itself—what scholars call the "common share meal," what moderns would call a potluck? Justin indicates thanksgiving over bread and wine cup only, with care for the hungry poor flowing from and following after the Eucharist. At the same time in North Africa, the early Christian teacher Tertullian described a Christian meal practice that focused on the poor. In contrast to the meals of the wealthy, this meal was kept in the "modest supper room" of Christians, a meal open to the many:

> Our feast explains itself by its name. The Greeks call it *agape* [that is, a feast of love]. Whatever it costs, our outlay in the name of piety is gain, since with the good things of the feast we benefit the needy; not as it is with you—[who] satisfy your licentious propensities in a belly-feast—but as it is with God himself, a peculiar respect is shown to the lowly. . . . As it is an act of religious service, it permits no vileness or immodesty. The participants, before reclining, taste first of prayer to God. As much is eaten as satisfies the cravings of hunger; as much is drunk as befits the chaste. . . . They talk as those who know that the Lord is one of their auditors. After manual ablution, and the bringing in of lights, each is asked to stand forth and sing a hymn to God, either one from the Holy Scriptures or one of his own composing. . . . As the feast commenced with prayer, so

> with prayer it is closed. We go from it, not like troops of mischief-doers, nor bands of vagabonds, nor to break out into licentious acts, but to have as much care of our modesty and chastity as if we had been at a school of virtue rather than a banquet.[12]

One Christian meal tradition, the one that would come to prevail in Christian sacramental practice, focused on the last supper Jesus held with some of his followers the night before his death. The identification of broken bread with a broken body and a cup of poured wine with spilled blood would be the means through which Christians connected the death of Jesus with food and drink: by eating the bread and drinking from the cup, one was drawn into the Lord's death and the mystery of redemption. This meal would come to be called the Lord's Supper, Eucharist, Holy Communion, and the Mass. On the other hand, the agape tradition described by Tertullian focused on the meal practice of Jesus during his life: his eating and drinking with social outcasts (Mark 2:13-17), his violation of Mosaic law so that the hungry could eat (Mark 2:23-28), the provision of food for hungry peasants (Mark 6:30-44), the wilderness feeding of four thousand (Mark 8:1-9), and his keeping the Passover meal and its memory of God's provision of food and drink for the destitute (Mark 14:17-25). In the agape tradition there were both the memory of Jesus' response to the hungry poor and the enactment of that practice in early Christian communities. Thus, for some time and in some places, early Christians kept a "martyr meal" in memory of Jesus' self-giving in death and an agape, a "poor meal," in memory of his sharing food and drink with outcasts and the hungry.

From the practice of recounting Jesus' sayings, telling stories about him, and keeping meal practices in his memory, there emerged among early Christians a series of social initiatives that responded to pressing human need. While other understandings of the person and mission of Jesus would abound in these centuries and the ones to come, images of Christ the servant, healer, and table host remained alive in the Christian assembly, in its various forms of leadership, and in what would become an organized and coordinated network of social initiatives. In defense of the Christian faith, the Christian teacher and philosopher Aristides of Athens offered a glowing description of Christian charity: "[Christians] do not despise widows and orphans," he wrote.

> The one who has [money] distributes to the one who has not. . . . When one of their poor passes away, they provide for burial according to their ability; and if they hear of any among them who are imprisoned or oppressed for the name of the Anointed One [Christ], all of them provide for his needs. . . . And if there is one who is poor and needy, they fast for two or three days that they may supply the needy with food. . . . But the good which they do, they do not boast of in the ears of the multitude [the general population]. . . . They hide their gift as the one who has found a treasure.[13]

It would seem that the striking and memorable practice of Jesus, a poor and wandering Palestinian Jew, had spilled outward into the complexity and distress of urban and Romanized life. Where his broken body was remembered in word and ritual act, communities and individuals promoted and supervised responses to those who suffered in society: the vulnerable newborn, the orphan, the homeless and hungry poor, the chronically ill and the plague victim, the aging widow, the dying, and the destitute with no one to bury them.

Patron of Orphans and Protector of the Poor

Nearly three hundred years after the death of Jesus of Nazareth, the emperor Constantine issued an edict in 313 that ordered tolerance for all religions, including Christianity. Whether or not Constantine received a vision from heaven that promised victory in battle "by the sign of the cross" matters little; one can only judge the discernable effects of such a vision. With remarkable alacrity, Constantine not only freed Christians from the threat of government persecution but also granted recompense to Christian communities whose liturgical books and biblical texts had been confiscated or destroyed in the Great Persecution at the beginning of the fourth century. He promised them the return of their "meeting houses" and the release of their clergy from the burden of public office so that they could tend to "the worship that they owe the Deity." Furthermore, he funded the building of the first Christian basilica—on the outskirts of Rome and named in honor of the Savior—and the construction of Christian basilicas in Roman

Palestine. Some sixty-eight years later, in 381, the emperor Theodosius proclaimed Christianity the approved religion of the state, an arrangement that would endure for close to 1,400 years—longer in some parts of the West and in the Christianized regions of the East.

Yet, at the very moment when Christianity became a legal and then state religion—when Christian communities emerged from a world of skepticism and open persecution—the dream of imperial unity began to unravel. By the late third century, the imperial army was contending with revolts in Britain and North Africa, an ongoing foreign war with Persia, and the growing power and destruction of Vandal, Visigothic, and Ostrogothic armies. So concerned was Constantine to be closer to the eastern provinces of the empire that he moved the seat of imperial power from Rome to the new city he built and named after himself: Constantinople, modern-day Istanbul. In the vacuum of political leadership created by the departure of the imperial court, the old aristocratic and senatorial families of Rome vied with each for political control of the city. The stunning and unimagined invasion and subsequent pillage of the "eternal city" in 410 by the Visigothic general Alaric demonstrated the fragility of the empire and the incompetence of aristocratic families to respond to military threats and the damage done to the social and economic infrastructure of the region.

There was, however, one person in the imperial capital who supervised a highly organized and tested network of communities scattered through the city: the bishop of Rome. While he was charged with the religious leadership of Christians in the city and the region, and would begin to claim a "primacy among equals" for the churches of Western Europe, the unsettling political context and disintegration of leadership in the West thrust him into a position of social and economic leadership previously unimagined. While early Christians had developed diverse responses to the poor and vulnerable in the context of urban misery, the unraveling of the economic, political, and social infrastructure of the western portion of the empire presented medieval Christians with new challenges. Into the vacuum of leadership created by government's abandonment of the people entered the bishop, the monk, and the nun.

In 590, a former city administrator was consecrated the bishop of Rome. Born into a senatorial family in 540, Gregory had abandoned his administrative and political duties by 574, sold his property, and given away his wealth in order to become a monk in an urban monastery. With other lay Christians of his time, he was deeply disturbed with what appeared to be the easy assimilation into Christianity of cultural values that he found at odds with his understanding of the faith. Did Christianity offer a comforting approval of life that was largely shaped by cultural views and practices, many of which seemed at odds with the teachings and practices of Jesus? Or did the call to follow Christ lead one in "the narrow way," into a pattern of life shaped by the One who held no property or wealth, who practiced an equitable sharing of goods, and who allied himself with the poor, the "little ones" beloved in the reign of God? It was thus with the greatest reluctance and after much interior struggle that Gregory accepted election as the bishop of Rome. Needless to say, he found Italy and much of the imperial West in an alarming state.

While Rome had once boasted the most sophisticated water system in the world, its aqueducts had fallen into ruin or been destroyed by invaders seeking to cut off water supplies to the city. Yet water continued to pour into the outlying regions and had created vast marshes soon filled with mosquitoes bearing waves of malaria into the city. With invading armies came the destruction of the vast road structure that served as the communications and commercial transportation network throughout the West. The transport of farm goods ground to a slow trickle. The agricultural estates of wealthy Christians, who had given their land as gifts to the church, fell into a state of disuse owing to poor supervision, intermittent raids, and a precipitous drop in population. Indeed, the imperial capital had boasted a population in the hundreds of thousands at the end of the third century, yet by the beginning of the sixth century, it had fallen below twenty thousand. Thus Rome, the peninsula, and large portions of the West were faced with the threat of famine, plague, invasion, and violent death; the chronic disruption of commercial trade; and the inability to respond to sickness, disease, or life-threatening wounds with any form of medical attention that actually alleviated suffering. One could beseech Christ and the martyrs to heal and save, yet people continued to starve and die of disease or lethal wounding.

In the context of social collapse, Gregory—charged with the spiritual leadership of Christians—emerged, first reluctantly and then forcefully, as a gifted economic and political leader. After all, the churches of Western Europe had followed the orderly pattern of the Roman Empire's organizational structure: in every key regional city there was a bishop; in the parishes of the region or diocese, priests and deacons served in local parishes; and in many a city and countryside, monastic communities of laywomen and laymen had begun to spring up. With no governmental assistance from the distant emperor in the East and little political assistance from the few remaining aristocratic families, Gregory supervised a network of social services that had existed in Christian communities since the first century. This well-organized administration was prepared to respond to the social crises that hurtled into people's lives on a regular basis.

Within weeks of his consecration as bishop, Gregory set about the drainage of the marshes outside the city so that a regular rotation of crops could be grown. He reformed the supervision of the church's farming estates by appointing ecclesial rectors who would ensure that produce was delivered to communities desperate for food. He asked that accurate bookkeeping be rigorously maintained to prevent cheating and to give an account of the growth or decline in crops. He directed deacons in their work among the poor, the sick, and the dying: no one was to starve, and no one was to be abandoned during the plague. Those who died in poverty were not to be thrown into anonymous pauper graves but receive the dignity of Christian burial. As Gregory once said to his secretary, "One should not promote the worldly interests of the church so much as the relief of the needy in their distress." Each afternoon, at the monastery he founded on Rome's Coelian Hill, he provided and shared a meal with a dozen poor people of the city so that he could come to know them and hear of their needs.[14]

While later generations of Christians would call for the reform of Christianity because too much attention had been given to promoting the "worldly interests of the church," Gregory used legal expertise, public administrative experience, supervision of lay monastics and ordained ministers, knowledge of scripture and liturgy, and an existing form of structured generosity to meet "the relief of the needy in their distress." In the midst of invasion, plague, and famine—and without any assistance from a distant government in the East—Gregory was able to invigorate and supervise the networks of Christian social service so that they could respond to the vulnerable and poor of his city and region. That he insisted on the provision of bread at the Eucharist and food for the hungry homeless did not appear to be two completely different things, one "spiritual" and one "material," but rather a continuum of care that responded to the whole person. The produce from farming estates was not to be used for the gain of Christ's ministers, he claimed, but Christ's own poor. By tending to the nutritional, medical, sanitary, and housing needs of the people in his "spiritual" charge, the bishop, with his deacons and monks, became the human face of God's providential care for "orphans and widows" (Ps. 68:5).

Gregory and his generation faced a great irony: as urban centers experienced diminishment and destruction, the many monastic centers located in the hinterland slowly and surely grew into a vast network of communities committed to the care of the poor and travelers, the sick, and the hungry. Gregory, who would come to be called "the Great," wrote the only existing life of Benedict of Nursia,[15] founder of the lay monastic movement that would eventually take his name, the Benedictines. In his hagiographical biography, Gregory portrayed a young man little different from himself. As a student of rhetoric in Rome, Benedict grew weary of endless carousing with his classmates. He sensed an uneasiness within himself not addressed by the camaraderie of fellow students or studies that would lead him to success. Refusing the prospects of an urban career, he left the city and became a solitary—a hermit—in the rocky hills east of Rome. Gregory notes that he spent many months in seclusion, praying and reflecting on the scriptures. In time, other young men joined him and formed a small community inspired by their reading of the Acts of the Apostles:

> They devoted themselves to the apostles' teaching and fellowship, to the breaking of bread and the prayers. . . . All who believed were together and had all things in common; they would sell their possessions and goods and distribute the proceeds to all, as any had need. Day by day, as they spent much time together in the temple, they broke bread at home and ate their food with glad and generous hearts, praising God and having the goodwill of all the people. (2:42-47)

As noted in the Rule that bears his name, Benedict envisioned the monastic life as a rhythm of communal prayer and communal work—*ora et labora*, prayer and labor. The daily schedule of the monastery was marked by seven times in which the monks or nuns would gather for worship: for the singing of the psalms, for prayer, and the proclamation of scripture. At the same time, the monastery was a place in which all those who entered would "sell their possessions and goods" and distribute the proceeds to the poor. As members of monastic community, monks or nuns "held all things in common." Each offered to the community what he or she could in terms of labor; each received what he or she needed in terms of food, shelter, and clothing. In other words, monastic communities practiced an equitable sharing of goods so that no one would be in want. Regardless of his or her status in the larger culture, the sharing of all things and being clothed in common vesture were intended to underscore the egalitarianism that Benedict discerned in the biblical description of the first Christian community.[16]

While early medieval monastic life kept a daily rhythm of communal prayer and Eucharist, a foretaste of sharing in the divine life, the Rule of Benedict also envisioned the monastery as a place of hospitality, especially for those in need. The monastery was a place of seclusion "from the world," yet it was also opened to the world. The Rule instructed all monks and nuns that "all guests who present themselves are to be welcomed as Christ, for he himself will say: *I was a stranger and you welcomed me* (Matt. 25:35). Proper honor must be shown *to all, especially to those who share our faith* (Gal. 6:10) and to pilgrims."[17] Since the monastery was the permanent home of monks or nuns, it was necessary to learn the many skills that would sustain a community: construction of buildings, forest and land supervision, crop and orchard management, food production and preparation, animal husbandry, and natural medicine. Although monastic life emerged as a challenging alternative to urban life, the monastery itself became a small "city" sustaining the monastic inhabitants with shelter, clothing, food, herbal medicine, sanitation, furniture, and tools. The monastery survived to the degree that its inhabitants could provide the necessities of life.

When combined with Benedict's admonition to welcome guests, relieve the poor, clothe the naked, visit the sick, and bury the dead,[18] the goods and the skills of the monastery were at the disposal of those in need. The turning of these secluded cloisters toward the vulnerable and needy who lived close by took place as the older economic, political, and social order was collapsing. Monastic hospitality became a form of service to real human need. Certainly the monastic life was interpreted by many as a preparation for the life of the world to come, for union with God: yet the Rule also pushed the monastic impulse toward this world and its pressing needs in times of social disorder.

Since monasteries had to provide food for the resident community, monks and nuns became expert in the cultivation of crops. The monastic almoner was responsible for distributing the monastery's alms to the poor and needy in the form of food produced in monastic fields and clothing from monastic storage. Monastic gardeners became expert herbalists and allowed their knowledge of natural medicines to be used among those who were weak and sick in the surrounding community. Monasteries included hospices in which travelers—but also the sick, the dying, and the elderly—found care in the form of simple bathing facilities, a clean robe or tunic, a bed often shared with others, meals, and plant-based pharmacopoeia drawn from the monastic garden. Clearly these monastic hospices were powerless in the face of severe illness or epidemic, yet they did offer one of the very few if not the only centers of health care for hundreds of years. Since one of the works of mercy counseled in the Rule was the obligation to bury the dead, those who died without means were given Christian burial and a grave.

As a place of refuge in a time of social upheaval and economic uncertainty, the monastery was a center of stability shaped by the steady rhythm of prayer and work. Although Benedict had turned away from the Roman city and embraced a life of seeming seclusion, he brought with him and imprinted upon the Rule the Roman virtues of order, stability, and moderation. These were to be welcomed within the monastery and to guide its life. By emphasizing order and stability, the monastery ensured a daily pattern of work that followed the rising and setting of the sun. Such order ensured that the basic needs of life could be met through common labor. By emphasizing moderation in life, Benedict insisted that human need should always be met—and met with a measure of flexibility: there were to be no extreme fasts and no lavish feasts. If a monk or visitor became ill, the Rule counseled an extra measure of wine or meat in order to strengthen the sick. There was to be enough, not less or more, to meet human need.

Thus, the monastery—marked by hospitality and order, prayer and work—became one of the few places in which the social virtues of early Christianity survived as Western Europe experienced the convulsive disintegration of the ancient empire and witnessed the birth of a "barbarian" Christian culture increasingly shaped by monastic missionaries, teachers, scribes, and artists. It is little wonder that in Gregory's hagiography of Benedict, the bishop portrayed the monk in a cave and a wilderness. After all, Elijah heard the voice of God calling to him while he took refuge in a cave (1 Kings 19), and Jesus announced his utter dependence on God during his forty-day testing in the wilderness (Matt. 4:1-11). In a time and place of desolation, so Gregory seemed to suggest, the wilderness was a place in which life, monastic life, could spring forth unexpectedly.[19] While the great imperial cities crumbled, the monastery flourished, transforming the desolate wilderness into a holy city, a place in which many trees grew, filled with "leaves for the healing of the nations" (Rev. 22:2).

Failure and Faithfulness

Of course all of this could go wrong. Indeed it did from the beginning. The disciples asked Jesus to send the hungry crowd away "so that they could buy something for themselves to eat" (Mark 6:35). Yet this was a gathering of impoverished peasants who would have had little means to purchase anything in the surrounding villages. His followers argued about who was the greatest among them (Mark 9:33-37) and asked to be seated on either side of him in his glory (Mark 10:32-45). Yet, in a reversal of culturally formed notions of power, he announced that whoever desires to be "great" must be a servant in the reign of God. When a blind man cried out for mercy, the disciples and the crowd ordered him to be silent. Jesus broke through their indifference and healed the man (Mark 10:46-52).

Paul was compelled to rebuke the Corinthian Christians because their meal practice reinforced social stratification: the wealthy had plenty to eat, while the poor were left with little or nothing (1 Cor. 11:17-34). On the one hand, the historical Paul commended women as leaders in the Christian community, as coworkers, deacons, and hosts (Rom. 16:1-16), yet only a few decades later the author of 1 Timothy urged Christians to "let a woman learn in silence with full submission. . . . Permit no woman to teach or to have authority over a man; she is to keep silent" (2:11-12). While the Synoptic Gospels and the letters of Paul offer glimpses of equitable sharing and egalitarian sensibilities, the author of James found it necessary to criticize Christians who, in their assembly, catered to the rich and demeaned the poor by expecting them to stand or to sit, a posture of subordination and shame (2:1-13). This was a discriminatory practice, one that abrogated the suspension of class status secured in Christian baptism.

While Dionysius, Cyprian, and Aristides portrayed Christians and their social initiatives as heroic and life-giving, there is also evidence that Christians hoarded in times of famine, ignored their suffering neighbors, abandoned each other in the face of persecution, and scorned the medically advanced health care provided by pagans. While wealthy Christians gave farm land to bishops as an ongoing source of assistance to the poor and needy, some bishops spent more energy on the "worldly interests of the church" than on care for "Christ's needy ones." Land as gift could readily become land as source of personal wealth. While many bishops took seriously their charge to be advocates of the voiceless poor and protectors of the weak, especially in times of economic prosperity the influence of wealthy families and the lure of monetary gain were powerful forces that distracted bishops and other church leaders from their care of the widow and the orphan, the hungry and the sick.

Likewise, the monastery, which at one time had struggled to survive, became proficient, prosperous, and then wealthy. For some communities and some abbots, the temptation was great to see such prosperity as a sign of God's favor, but, then, what of the poor? While Benedict's Rule envisioned the monastic community as a center of hospitality—a Christian space opened to people in a society crumbling under invasion—numerous monasteries became centers of astonishing wealth. A monk or nun was never allowed to own anything of his or her own, but this did not prevent communities from growing rich on the produce of their farmlands—lands owned by abbeys but frequently tilled and harvested by poor serfs. Indeed, one medieval cartoon shows a ravenous wolf disguised as an obese monk eating an entire sheep and then munching on a house in the presence of a widow and an orphan. The two frail figures, a third the size of the monk, stand before him with hands upraised in supplication.[20] While such an image did not represent all monastic communities, monastic wealth became an object of ridicule: How could those devoutly pledged to imitate the life of Christ, poor and property-less, ignore his obvious concern for the needy?

The indifference of Christian businesspeople to manifest human suffering during the commercial renaissance of the high Middle Ages inspired Francis and Clare of Assisi to abandon their lives of privilege in order to follow the poor Christ among the hungry and the sick, the leper and the dying.[21] And yet many Franciscans—vowed to Lady Poverty—enshrined the dead Francis in a basilica of magnificent proportions and soon found themselves quarreling over property rights rather than the rights or needs of the poor. At the same time, lay confraternities sprang up to assist the chronically sick and the indigent. Nevertheless, a generation or two later, their prowess at raising funds would benefit only their members, the beggar and the displaced peasant overlooked and forgotten.[22]

While early and medieval Christians created and sustained social initiatives among the poor and vulnerable, and while they adapted such initiatives in light of new threats to human wholeness and health, they were not immune to a self-preserving impulse. After all, it was much easier to offer coins to the hungry homeless than welcome them into one's home for a meal; the chance might be too great that one would discover a real human being rather than the frightening visage of a nameless beggar. While priests and religious sisters ministered tirelessly among the victims of the Black Plague in the fourteenth century, wealthy lay Christians fled the cities into the relative security of the countryside. Church leaders consistently encouraged the faithful to give alms—handouts—to the poor. Yet these same leaders found it difficult to ask *why* one needed to give alms in the first place. Indeed, was it not helpful to have a permanent class of the needy and vulnerable at hand? After all, one could always offer them *something* in the name of Christ and still cling to one's material securities. Evidence also exists, however, of bishops, priests, and monks who preached clearly and pointedly that the keeping of much by the few while the many were left destitute was a flagrant violation of God's intentions that all created things be shared among all creatures for their sustenance.[23]

Both faithfulness and failure have marked the entire course of the church's history. While one might search for it, there is no "golden age" when Christian social initiatives reflected a brighter glow. Early and medieval Christians failed and succeeded in their offers of companionship, nourishment, and healing to "the least in the reign of God." It was in the dialectical pull, in that tension between failure and faithfulness, between self-preservation and care for the other, that the *diakonia* of Christ was exercised in house church, agape meal, nursing care, basilica, hospice, orphanage, poor house, cathedral, hospital, and monastery. Amid failures grievous and petty, the West was nonetheless drawn toward public care of the suffering, drawn by the invitations and instructions of Jesus read in the liturgy and celebrated in the sacraments:

> Come, you that are blessed by my Father, inherit the kingdom prepared for you from the foundation of the world; for I was hungry and you gave me food, I was thirsty and you gave me something to drink, I was a stranger and you welcomed me, I was naked and

> you gave me clothing, I was sick and you took care of me, I was in prison and you visited me. (Matt. 25:34-36)

From Norway to the southern tip of Italy, from France to the eastern reaches of Poland, Christ's invitation was to be found in medieval wall paintings, tapestries, sculpture, and carvings—the buildings and their artwork proclaiming that the One worshipped within was among the little ones of this earth, waiting with open hands.

For Further Reading

Brown, Peter. *The Rise of Western Christendom*. 2nd ed. Oxford: Blackwell, 2003.

Cahill, Thomas. *How the Irish Saved Civilization: The Untold Story of Ireland's Heroic Role from the Fall of Rome to the Rise of Medieval Europe*. New York: Doubleday, 1995.

Constable, Giles. *The Reformation of the Twelfth Century*. Cambridge: Cambridge University Press, 1996.

Krautheimer, Richard. "The Times of Gregory the Great." In *Rome: Profile of a City, 312–1308*, 59–88. Princeton: Princeton University Press, 2002.

Lawrence, C. H. *Medieval Monasticism*. Essex: Pearson Education, 2001.

Markus, R. A. *Gregory the Great and His World*. Cambridge: Cambridge University Press, 1997.

Meeks, Wayne A. *The Origins of Christian Morality: The First Two Centuries*. New Haven: Yale University Press, 1993.

Mollat, Michel. *The Poor in the Middle Ages*. Trans. Arthur Goldhammer. New Haven: Yale University Press, 1990.

Stark, Rodney. *The Rise of Christianity: How the Obscure, Marginal Jesus Movement Became the Dominant Religious Force in the Western World in a Few Centuries*. San Francisco: HarperSanFrancisco, 1997.

3

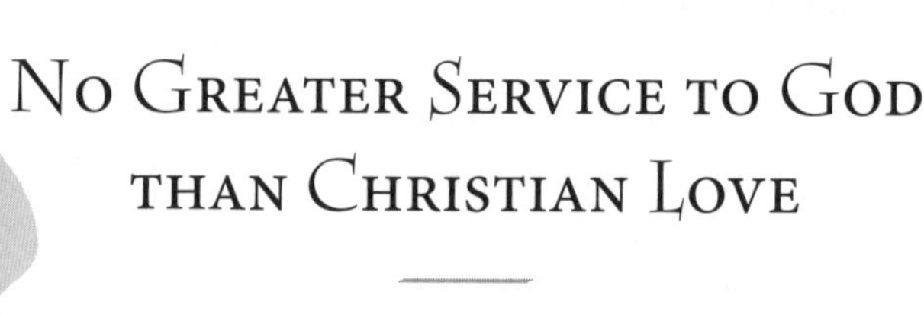

No Greater Service to God than Christian Love

Insights from Martin Luther

Carter Lindberg

Martin Luther has been portrayed in numerous ways, often tinted by social and political conservatism but rarely as a social activist. Yet social and political activism was integral to his pastoral and theological life and thought. While some of his contributions to the social issues of his day are available in specific tracts, most are interwoven throughout his writings. It is important to remember that Luther did not understand himself to be a social reformer, but rather a pastor and professor of scripture. Hence, as we reflect upon his contributions to social ethics, it behooves us to begin by reviewing in brief his theological basis for social ethics.

Luther succinctly defined theology in his commentary on Psalm 51: "The proper subject of theology is man guilty of sin and condemned, and God the Justifier and Savior of man the sinner. Whatever is asked or discussed in theology outside this subject is error and poison."[1] He provided a mini systematic exposition of his definition in his "Preface to the Epistle of St. Paul to the Romans."[2] The gist of Luther's theology is that justification is received as a free gift rather than achieved by the sinner's efforts. Salvation, then, is the foundation of life rather than its goal. The liberating news of this proclamation for social ethics is that faith active in love is not dependent upon its results. In relation to his definition of theology, Luther also described the Christian as "simultaneously sinner and righteous." He thereby acutely realized the ambiguities in all social, political activity. Christians, too, have hidden and mixed motives.

While neither the Augsburg Confession nor the writings of Luther provide us with a road map to social service, they may function to orient our position and direction with the following compass points:

1. Christians are called to responsible service *in* the world, socially and politically as well as in other ways, for the sake of the well-being of others.

2. The distinction between "spiritual" and "secular" authorities in Luther's writings and the Augsburg Confession is intended to facilitate, not hinder, this responsible service. The key here is Luther's well-known distinction—but not separation!—of law and gospel as distinct modes of God's activity to preserve and redeem creation.

3. The gospel is the unequivocal promise that our destiny with God is God's own free gift and is not contingent on our works. Since our certainty of redemption does not derive from what we do but rather from what God has done, we are emancipated

- from the fear and anxiety that accompanies grounding our security in political and social works;
- from all forms of political messianism or millenarianism that equate the kingdom of God with particular political and social programs;
- for political realism and the courage to "sin boldly" in carrying out our political and social responsibilities;
- for the consolation of the gospel, which not only encourages us to assume public responsibilities but also comforts our consciences and those of our leaders in the midst of the ambiguities inherent in choices made in a fallen world.

4. The theological use of the law exposes our sin even in our good works and opens our eyes to our own contributions to creation's groaning and travail. In its own way God's judgment also emancipates us

- from the illusion that any political and social decision or action may be unambiguous and righteous;
- for political and social decisions and actions without the self-deception and the self-righteousness that Christians as Christians

have any special expertise above and beyond that available to anyone of reason and good will.

5. The civil or political use of the law, which works to restrain evil and support human community, is operative everywhere in the world in one form or another as the principle of order. This universality of the law also emancipates us

- from requiring agreement in doctrine, be it theological or political, before cooperation toward achieving limited objectives beneficial to the common good;
- for recognition of the role of power in the political and social pursuit of peace and order;
- for negotiation for the common good on the basis of mutual self-interest because our concern is societal well-being, not our own moral purity;
- for the critical use of reason to achieve the political goal of earthly welfare.

These abstractions of the resources of our Lutheran tradition reflect the theme of Christian freedom (cf. "The Freedom of a Christian"[3]). This theme—so eloquently expressed by Luther's dictum that the Christian is at one and the same time a perfectly free lord of all, subject to no one, and a perfectly dutiful servant of everyone, subject to everyone—is a timely orientation in the face of the utopian paths and dystopian chasms surrounding the issues of social and economic justice. It directs us to the freedom that liberates us from both the illusion that the next technological or social breakthrough will save us and the despair that social catastrophe is just around the corner. It is this freedom for responsible and intelligent action in the world for the world that is expressed in the Augsburg Confession and in Luther's theology.

The Christian is to take seriously the task of world building and the maintenance of culture, society, and civilization, but always with the conviction that every culture, every system of justice, and every political structure is only relative and instrumental for the humanization of people. Tradition is to be conserved with insight into its dehumanizing aspects and its penultimacy. Reason and love are to be active in the continual task of socialization in the recognition that God—not the law, not the past, not the state, not even the church—is sovereign in history. For Luther, faith alone grants the security to live within the human insecurity of relative structures. It is only by faith that persons can avoid the defensive sanctification of past, present, or future goods and values. Faith is the enabling ground of the person who is content to be human and to let God be God.

In light of the above, I shall sketch Luther's contributions under the following heuristic designations (these are not Luther's but are used as an organizational tool for the purposes of this essay): worship and social service; government and social welfare; government regulation of the economy; preaching to "unmask" social injustice and to lobby for social justice.

The "Liturgy after the Liturgy": Worship and Social Service

The phrase "liturgy after the liturgy" aptly expresses Luther's conviction that worship and social ethics are inseparable, a conviction reiterated by the pioneer of modern German diaconal studies, Paul Philippi, who emphasized that the reality of *diaconia* flows from the real presence.[4] Luther began treating the relationship of worship and social ethics quite early. Already in 1519, his tract "The Blessed Sacrament of the Holy and True Body of Christ, and the Brotherhoods" appeared and was followed in 1520 by "A Treatise on the New Testament, That Is, the Holy Mass."[5] Both were written in German (thus addressed to the laity), and both set forth ecclesiological and sacramental foundations for social ethics.

The keynote of the sacrament is solidarity. Just as Christ is really present for us, so we are formed into a community of love that is really present for its members. "Through the interchange of his [Christ's] blessings and our misfortunes, we become one loaf, one bread, one body, one drink, and have all things in common." "This fellowship is twofold: on the one hand we partake of Christ and all saints; on the other hand we permit all Christians to be partakers of us, in whatever way they and we are able."[6]

Luther develops his point by analogy to urban life: "Christ and all saints are one spiritual body, just as the inhabitants of a city are one community and body, each citizen being a member of the other and of the entire city."[7] Sharing with Christ means sharing everything, including "suffering and sins." In contrast to contemporary visions of either urban anomie and despair or the liberation of the "secular city," Luther presents communal life informed by faith active in love. The fellowship of the communion of saints is like

> a city where every citizen shares with all the others the city's name, honor, freedom, trade, customs, usages, help, support, protection, and the like, while at the same time he shares all the dangers of fire and flood, enemies and death, losses, taxes, and the like. . . . Here we see that whoever injures one citizen injures an entire city and all its citizens; whoever benefits one [citizen] deserves favor and thanks from all the others. . . . This is obvious: if anyone's foot hurts him, yes, even the little toe, the eye at once looks at it, the fingers grasp it, the face puckers, the whole body bends over to it, and all are concerned with this small member; again, once it is cared for all the other members are benefited. This comparison must be noted well if one wishes to understand this sacrament, for Scripture uses it for the sake of the unlearned.[8]

Paul Philippi provides an equally graphic analogy for the real presence: it is like the entire congregation breathing in and out. The inhaling of the offering of Christ in the sacrament leads to the exhaling of distributing gifts in the community.[9] To belabor the obvious: one cannot exhale without inhaling. Hence the logic of the placement of Articles 5 and 6 of the Augsburg Confession. The gospel and sacraments are the means through which the Holy Spirit works faith; faith effects love, and love does good works.

Worship, for Luther, is real communion with Christ and the congregation. So he appeals to the material understanding of fellowship in the early church where the real presence led to collecting food and goods for the poor. "We have a vestige of this [practice] in the little word 'collect' in the mass, which means a general collection, just as a communion fund is gathered to be given to the poor. . . . [Then] Christians cared for one another, supported one another, bore one another's burdens and affliction. This has all disappeared, and now there remain only the many masses and the many who receive this sacrament without in the least understanding or practicing what it signifies."[10] In his "Treatise on the New Testament," Luther continued to appeal to the ancient church's gathering of food, money, and necessities in connection with the Mass for distribution to the poor.[11]

We are, Luther emphasizes, to pay close attention to the word "sacrifice," or "offering," "so that we do not presume to give God something in the sacrament, when it is he who in it give us all things. . . . What sacrifices, then, are we to offer? Ourselves, and all that we have, with constant prayer." From scripture "we learn that we do not offer Christ as a sacrifice, but that Christ offers us."[12] God does not need our gifts, but the neighbor does. The communion of saints is thus not only in the reception of God's gift in the sacrament but also in the mutual self-offering to each other. "Wherefore this sacrament is rightly called 'a fountain of love.'"[13] "Now there is no greater service of God [*Dienst gottis*, "service of God"; note that *Gottesdienst* means "worship service"] than Christian love which helps and serves the needy, as Christ himself will judge and testify at the Last Day, Matthew 25[:31-46]."[14]

Luther's concept of "offering" bridges worship and social ethics, and it reminds us that both worship and social ethics are communal. Paul Rorem's suggestion that church exit signs be labeled "servants' entrance" concisely conveys Luther's conviction that communal service to the neighbor is the continuation of worship in the world, that social ethics is the liturgy after the liturgy.[15] "The fruit of the sacrament . . . is nothing other than love. . . . As he gave himself for us with his body and blood in order to redeem us from all misery, so we too are to give ourselves with might and main for our neighbor. . . . That is how a Christian acts. He is conscious of nothing else than that the goods which are his are also given to his neighbor. He makes no distinction but helps everyone with body and life, goods and honor, as much as he can."[16] While this is certainly a statement of personal commitment, it is by no means to be read privatistically. Those who rail against government programs of social welfare under the shibboleth of "personal responsibility" may be surprised to learn that Luther was one of the first powerful advocates for tax-supported government welfare programs.

Social Welfare Policies and Legislation

By the eve of the Reformation, worship and welfare were no longer the inseparable expression of the community that "holds all in common" (Acts 4:32). Poverty had become a major social problem comprising a complex of issues involved with the rise of a profit economy. The new economic developments of the late medieval period exacerbated widespread poverty, vagrancy, and underemployment. The urban tax registers indicate that the so-called have-nots ranged from 30 to 75 percent of the population. In addition there were major fluctuations of this widespread poverty because large numbers of day laborers existed on a subsistence level, always a day away from mendicancy. Practical efforts to restrain the near omnipresence of begging were frustrated by a theological ideology that legitimated begging and valued almsgiving. In religious terms, the poor had an important soteriological function as intercessors for almsgivers, and at the same time, the poor were a cheap labor pool for an expanding profit economy. In this context, the medieval schema of salvation that presented poverty as the ideal of Christian life—and promised earthly and heavenly rewards to the almsgiver—inhibited recognition and alleviation of the social distress of poverty.

One of the great French Dominican preachers of Luther's time, Guillaume Pepin (1465–1533), explained the inequalities of economic life in terms of the medieval ideology of almsgiving and salvation. "Why does God want some in this world to be rich and others poor? . . . I say that God has till now ordained that some are rich and others poor, so that each one has the material at hand to merit the kingdom of God. The rich by giving alms to the poor, the poor by patiently doing their work, and praying that the rich will sustain them."[17] The rich could buy salvation with charity. Even Juan Luis Vives, the Spanish Catholic humanist known for his effort to provide an impetus to civic welfare among other things, repeated this mantra that there is a "heavenly reward . . . prepared as a recompense for almsgiving that proceeds from charity."[18] These examples are among many that reflect the long tradition stemming from the early church fathers' use of such apocryphal writings as Tobit (4:9-11; 12:9—"almsgiving delivers from death") and Ecclesiasticus (3:30—"almsgiving atones for sin") and the Augustinian-Thomistic heritage of "faith formed by love" (*caritas*, charity), which focused on the salvatory merit accruing to the donor that atoned for sin, enabled philanthropy, and transferred one's wealth to heaven.

Luther's doctrine of justification by grace alone, apart from works, cut the nerve of this medieval ideology of poverty. Salvation is received—not achieved—and thus salvation is the foundation for life rather than its goal.

Since salvation is purely God's gift, both poverty and almsgiving lose soteriological significance. Furthermore, this also undercut the explanatory function of the medieval ideology of poverty that fatalistically presented poverty and riches as the divine plan. By despiritualizing poverty, the Reformers could recognize poverty in all its forms as a personal and social evil to be combated. Under the rubrics of justice and equity, Luther and his colleagues quickly moved in alliance with local governments to establish new social welfare policies.

The first major effort in this direction was the Wittenberg Church Order of 1522, which established a "common chest" for welfare work. Initially funded by the expropriation of medieval ecclesiastical endowments and later by taxes, the Wittenberg Order prohibited begging; provided interest-free loans to artisans, who when established were to repay them if possible; provided for poor orphans, the children of poor people, and poor women who needed an appropriate dowry for marriage; provided refinancing of high-interest loans at 4 percent annual interest for burdened citizens; and supported the education or vocational training of poor children. To the objection that this was open to abuse, Luther replied, "He who has nothing to live should be aided. If he deceives us, what then? He must be aided again."[19] Other communities quickly picked up these ideas. By 1523 there were common chest provisions for social welfare in the church orders of Leisnig, Augsburg, Nuremberg, Altenburg, Kitzingen, Strasbourg, Breslau, and Regensburg. Luther's colleague Johannes Bugenhagen was instrumental in creating similar legislation, including the establishment of public schools throughout northern German cities as well as Denmark. The incipient conception of the welfare state entailed contributions from everyone able to contribute, and understood the reception of support not as charity but as a social right.

These ordinances for poverty relief were efforts to implement Luther's conviction that social welfare policies designed to prevent as well as remedy poverty are a Christian social responsibility. Under the motto "there should be no beggars among Christians," the Reformation movement set about implementing concern for personal dignity and public alleviation of suffering. Luther and his colleagues taught that the giving of alms was no longer bound up with appeasement for sin, redemption, or expectation of divine reward, but rather that faith active in love is expressed in regulated, centralized, and communally supported and administered social welfare.

GOVERNMENT REGULATION OF THE ECONOMY

Luther's sustained and virulent attack on the works righteousness of the medieval ladder of virtues was equally an attack on the early profit economy—in our terms, the corporate ladder. Both reveal the drive to secure one's existence, and as such they express the counterfeit gospel that a person's worth depends upon achievement. To Luther, the good news is that human worth is independent of success, whether it is measured in terms of renunciation or acquisition of the world. Luther therefore fought a two-sided battle against monastic asceticism on the one hand and early modern capitalism on the other hand. The first battle is far better known than the second. Luther viewed both the monastic drive to renounce the world and the capitalist drive to acquire the world as two sides of the same coin—salvation by works. The problem, Luther noted, is not money but its use. The greedy misuse the world by striving to acquire it, the monastics by struggling to renounce it.[20] The end result for both is personal insecurity because trust is placed in self-achievement rather than in God. Meanwhile the neighbor is neglected.

Some scholars have argued that Luther was a political and social conservative whose theology promoted subservience to political authorities and an ethical quietism. But if Luther was so conservative, how do we account for his lifelong criticism of early capitalism as a *systemic* injustice, his call for government regulation of business and banking, and his contribution to social welfare legislation? A list of some of his writings shows his engagement with the burning financial and welfare issues of his day. (Then as now, printers were interested in profit; hence the publication numbers of Luther's tracts indicate their popularity.) Luther attacked profiteering in the "Short Sermon on Usury" (1519), appearing in three editions, and the "Long Sermon on Usury" (1520), both of which were incorporated into his major attack on early capitalism in his 1524 tract, "Trade and Usury,"[21] which appeared in seven editions.

People looked to Luther for guidance on economic reform and welfare issues. In 1523, in response to the request of the Leisnig town council, Luther wrote the preface to the town's "Ordinance of a Common Chest," which provided legislation for social welfare.[22] In 1525 the Danzig town council requested his advice on profiteering and legitimate interest rates. Luther's response emphasized equity and a limit of interest to 5 percent.

In the meantime, he wrote "To the Christian Nobility of the German Nation" (1520), in which he proclaimed that taking interest is the work of the devil and the greatest misfortune of the German nation, and he exhorted civil authorities to create social welfare programs.[23] He continued with "The Freedom of a Christian" (1520); "Temporal Authority: To What Extent It Should Be Obeyed" (1523); and "To the Councilmen of All Cities in Germany That They Establish and Maintain Christian Schools" (1524)—not to mention his biblical and sermon commentaries, for example, on Deut. 15:4, that there should be no poor among you (1525);[24] his exposition of the seventh commandment in his "Treatise on Good Works" (1520)[25] and the Large Catechism (1529); and his commentaries on the Magnificat (1521), the Sermon on the Mount (1532), and the Psalms. Finally, there is the explosive tract at the end of his life that exhorts pastors to excommunicate usurers, "Exhortation to the Clergy to Preach against Usury" (1540[26]), which went through four editions plus a translation into Latin. His criticism of the tax policies of the German princes and his promotion of fairer tax rates were deemed radical enough to be omitted from the Wittenberg edition of his writings.[27]

Yet, in spite of the fact that Luther's writings on economics were important to his contemporaries, these writings are today largely neglected. There are inexpensive editions of his 1520 tracts but not of "Trade and Usury." And his last effort, exhorting excommunication of laissez-faire capitalists, is largely unknown and available only in German, and then only in the Weimar, Erlangen, and Walch editions. It is not particularly surprising that American Lutherans are unaware of this side of Luther; after all, their society extols capitalism to the extent that CEOs receive hundreds of times the income of their employees, credit card companies make tens of billions in profits, and government administrations wash their hands of social justice by deregulating businesses and contributing to their excesses. There may be little interest in Luther's political-economic writings because they condemn the American way of life as conceived by those who attribute social problems to government regulations and programs and who extol free enterprise and its trickle-down philanthropy.

To counter that pervasive power with subsidy programs, even run by faith-based caregivers, does not begin to approach justice. At best, governmental faith-based initiatives echo the inadequacies of medieval almsgiving, that is, a Band-Aid approach that ignores systemic injustices; at worst they are a cynical means to gain votes from the Christian Right and to cut the domestic budget.[28] Indeed, there are uncomfortable parallels to Luther's context. As Barbara Ehrenreich notes, "the 'working poor,' as they are approvingly termed, are in fact the major philanthropists of our society. . . . They endure privation so that inflation will be low and stock prices high. To be a member of the working poor is to be an anonymous donor, a nameless benefactor, to everyone else."[29]

The medieval ideology of voluntary poverty as the privileged path to salvation had been entrenched for centuries, but the idea that money can make money was relatively new in the Reformation period. The medieval church's condemnation of the profit economy, termed "usury" in theology and canon law, was reiterated as late as the Fifth Lateran Council in 1515. But by then the entrepreneur was well established. Hence the popular saying, "Bürgen soll man würgen"—roughly translated: loan sharks should be strangled.

Luther detested the calculating entrepreneur. He was convinced that the new profit economy divorced money from use for human needs, necessitated an economy of acquisition, and nourished sin. Luther consistently preached and wrote against the expanding money and credit economy as a great sin. "After the devil there is no greater human enemy on earth than a miser and usurer for he desires to be God over everyone. Turks, soldiers, and tyrants are also evil men, yet they must allow the people to live. . . . Indeed, they must now and then be somewhat merciful. But a usurer and miser-belly desires that the entire world be ruined in order that there be hunger, thirst, misery, and need so that he can have everything and so that everyone must depend upon him and be his slave as if he were God."[30] "The poor are defrauded every day, and new burdens and higher prices are imposed. They all misuse the market in their own arbitrary, defiant, arrogant way, as if it were their privilege and right to sell their goods as high as they please without any criticism" (Large Catechism, seventh commandment).

The "lust for profit," Luther observed, had many clever expressions: selling on time and credit, manipulating the market by withholding or dumping goods, developing cartels and monopolies, falsifying bankruptcies, trading in futures, and just plain misrepresenting goods.[31] Luther's shorthand for these practices was "usury," the common medieval term for lending at interest. However, the focus of Luther's attack was not the medieval concept of usury, per se, but the financial practices related to large-scale national and international commerce.

Such usury, Luther argued, affects everyone. "The usury that occurs in Leipzig, Augsburg, Frankfurt, and other comparable cities is felt in our market and our kitchen. The usurers are eating our food and drinking our drink." Even worse, however, is that by manipulating prices, "usury lives off the bodies of the poor."[32] In his inimitable style, Luther exploded: "The world is one big whorehouse, completely submerged in greed," where the "big thieves hang the little thieves."[33] In his exposition of the seventh commandment (Large Catechism) Luther wrote, "Yes, we might well keep quiet here about individual petty thieves since we ought to be attacking the great, powerful archthieves with whom lords and princes consort and who daily plunder not just a city or two, but all of Germany. . . . Those who can steal and rob openly are safe and free, unpunished by anyone, even desiring to be honored." When Luther exhorted pastors to condemn usury as stealing and murder, and to refuse absolution, the sacrament, and Christian burial to usurers unless they repent, he had in mind "the great, powerful archthieves," not the "petty thieves" who fill prisons.[34]

The context for Luther's call to excommunicate profiteers was a plague of mice that destroyed crops in 1538 and the spring drought of 1539, which led to a steep rise in food prices and a famine in Wittenberg and surrounding areas.[35] Grain was being held off the market in order to gain higher prices. Luther requested communal assistance from the city council and received the reply that it was not responsible. He then appealed to Prince Johann Friedrich, pointing out that grain had been kept off the market "to the ruin of your electoral grace's land and people."[36] The following Sunday he preached against the avarice of the usurers. "They were all to be cursed and damned for they are the greatest enemies of the land" and "are strangling many people with shameful miserliness and usury." In order to spread his criticism as widely as possible, he wrote a pamphlet exhorting pastors to preach against the usurers.

Luther's concern was not merely about an individual's use of money but about the structural social damage inherent in the idolatry of the "laws" of the market. Ideas of an impersonal market and autonomous laws of economics were abhorrent to Luther because he saw them as both idolatrous and socially destructive. A recent essay analyzes "how much the market has become religiously exalted in our contemporary world. Like God, the market seems to be omnipotent, omniscient and omnipresent."[37] Luther saw the entire community endangered by the financial power of a few great economic centers. His concern is reflected in the saying of the day that "a bit should be placed in the mouth of the Fuggers,"[38] the central bank of the empire at that time. The rising world economy was already beginning to absorb urban and local economies and to increase opposition between rich and poor. He saw that economic coercion—we call it globalization—was immune to normal jurisdiction and thus perceived early capitalism as a "weapon of mass destruction" aimed at the common good, the ethos of community. That viewpoint is why Luther considered early capitalism to constitute a *status confessionis* for the church—a confessional not just an ethical issue—in spite of the fact that many of his contemporaries thought he was tilting at windmills.[39]

Luther believed that the church was called publicly and unequivocally not only to reject the destructive elements of the growing profit economy but also to develop a constructive social ethic in response to them. He and his colleagues promoted public accountability of large business through government regulation. Here Luther is not rejecting the profit economy out of hand, but rather promoting government control that would limit the interest rate to 5 percent in contrast to the 30 to 40 percent that was common in his time. Luther proposed a state-regulated economy that could enact price controls. For Luther, the biblical call to love the neighbor is expressed in society by justice and equity.

While Luther's efforts to develop welfare legislation were well received in the cities and territories that accepted the Reformation, his efforts to encourage civic control of capitalism did not gain comparable support. Of course, it is hardly surprising that when interest rates could soar to 40 percent, bankers turned a deaf ear to his call for a 5 percent ceiling on interest. Also, Luther's criticism of capitalism included far more than exorbitant interest rates. He argued that social need always stood above personal gain: "In a well-arranged commonwealth the debts of the poor who are in need ought to be cancelled, and they ought to be helped; hence the action of collecting has its place only against the lazy and the ne'er-do-well."[40]

Luther experienced that it is easier to motivate assistance to individuals than it is to curb the economic practices that create their poverty. Poverty's squalor calls out for redress, whereas the attractive trappings of business muffle criticism. Yet the effects of early capitalism could be felt, and the common good was being undermined by the activities of large businesses that could not be held accountable even by the emperor. In Wittenberg between 1520 and 1538 prices doubled, but wages remained the same. Luther called this disguised murder and robbery. "How skillfully Sir Greed can dress up to look like a pious man if that seems to be what the occasion requires, while he is actually a double scoundrel and a liar."[41] Indeed, "greed has a very pretty and attractive cover for its shame; it is called provision for the body and the needs of nature. Under this cover greed insatiably amasses unlimited wealth."[42] "God opposes usury and greed yet no one realizes this because it is not simple murder and robbery. Rather usury is a more diverse, insatiable murder and robbery. . . . Thus everyone should see to his worldly and spiritual office as commanded to punish the wicked and protect the pious."[43]

In his 1525 advice to the town council of Danzig, Luther stated that government regulation of interest should be according to the principle of equity. For example, a mortgage of 5 percent would be equitable, but it should be reduced if it does not yield this return. At the same time, one should consider the individual's personal economic situation. The well-to-do could be induced to waive a part of his interest, whereas an old person without means should retain it.[44]

But these views were of minimal influence. Legislation introduced in Dresden in 1529 prohibited 15 to 20 percent interest in favor of a 5 percent rate, in turn influencing the reform of the Zwickau city laws in 1539. Yet it was also noted how often such legislation was violated. That these examples may indicate more failure than success is confirmed by the 1564–65 controversy in Rudolstadt. The Lutheran pastor there refused to commune two parishioners who lived by usury. The theological faculties of Wittenberg, Leipzig, and Jena were requested to give their opinions. They concluded against the pastor, who then had to leave town, and they did not recognize Luther as an authority on this issue. After this there was never again a serious effort to acknowledge Luther's position on capitalism.

Luther's efforts to turn the early capitalist world upside down by insisting on government regulation of business was countered by the powerful of his day, the analogues to the CEOs of today's financial, energy, and pharmaceutical industries. Luther was not utopian in these matters. Nevertheless, throughout his career Luther fought against what he saw as the two-sided coin of mammonism: ascetic flight from money and the acquisitive drive for it. His foundation for this battle was the good news that a person's worth is not determined by what he or she does or does not possess, but rather by God's promise in Christ.

That is the gospel. But Luther held gospel and law together in dialectical tension. The gospel is for "despairing consciences," and the theological use of the law is for "hard and stubborn minds." The "glue" for civil society, however, is what Luther perceived as the civil or political use of the law, God's law of equity and justice. That law is written on the hearts of humankind, and its use is to restrain evil and promote the common good. It finds positive expression through the use of reason. So, for example, Luther emphasized that it is not necessary for social well-being that the emperor be Christian but that he be able to reason. "Christians are not needed for secular authority. Thus it is not necessary for the emperor to be a saint. It is not necessary for him to be a Christian to rule. It is sufficient for the emperor to possess reason."[45] Thus, it stands to reason that an ounce of prevention is worth a pound of cure.

Unfortunately, the American federal government is typically against prophylactic measures, whether they apply to economics or to sex. We may simply illustrate this by the old maxim that it is better to teach a person to fish than to give her a fish; in contemporary terms this is the "leave no fisherperson behind" mantra. But what does such "compassionate conservatism" say about mercury levels in the fish we catch or the actions that put such poisons in the environment or the globalization of fishing that corners the fish market?

Preaching to Unmask Evil and to Lobby for Social Justice

Pastors are to preach against the "great sin and shame" of usury that is ruining and destroying Germany. They are to make it clear that those who take more than 5 percent profit in interest are idolatrous servants of mammon and shall not be blessed unless they repent. Preachers should stand firm against the rejoinder that if the taking of interest is condemned, then "nearly the whole world would be damned." For the practice of the world contradicts the law and the Word of God, and therefore one is not to preach according to the customs of the world but must express what the law demands and should be done.[46] In the case of famine, the civil authority has to intervene, since refusal to sell grain is equivalent to stealing and robbing. What is done against God's Word and valid law is never a good deed, and the preachers should clearly say so. Luther did not naively assume that the CEOs of his day would change their ways. "We preachers can easily counsel but no one or few follow."[47] If it is said that the world cannot be without usury, this is true. But Christ says, woe to the person by whom offense comes (Matt. 18:7), and Luther concludes, "There must be usury, but woe to the usurer!"[48]

The preaching office is thus responsible to expose sin: to unmask economic injustice and its perpetrators. "Christ has instructed us preachers not to withhold the truth from the lords but to exhort and chide them in their injustice. . . . Then they say to us, 'You are reviling the majesty of God,' to which we answer, 'We will suffer what you do to us, but to keep still and let it appear that you do right when you do wrong, that we cannot and will not do.' We must confess the truth and rebuke the evil."[49]

Luther understood himself as a pastor and theologian—not as a politician—but this in no way minimized or limited his pastoral and theological concern for the secular realm of political decisions and involvement. The effects of political decisions on persons were included as an essential component of the commission to proclaim the gospel to the world and to emphasize to persons in their various positions of authority their obligations and responsibilities to their neighbors. Luther understood every political problem as a religious challenge that must be investigated in terms of its expression of the will of God.

Thus the religious challenge of political problems was to be met in the pulpit. The role of the preaching office, in addition to proclaiming the gospel, Luther argued, is, through preaching the law, to unmask hidden evils so that they may be addressed by the state. Luther epitomized what is known in classical and biblical studies as "frank speech." He did not hesitate to apply his "apocalyptic strategy of exposure by confrontation" in the pulpit as well as in tracts for the time. For Luther a function of preaching is "to unmask *hidden* injustice, thus saving the souls of duped Christians and opening the eyes of the secular authorities for their mandate to establish *civil* justice."[50] As Doug Marlette, the late Pulitzer Prize–winning editorial cartoonist for the *Atlanta Constitution*, noted, a healthy society depends upon the freedom to express ideas and opinions. A common denominator of all dictators and CEOs is the awareness that information is power. If you can control the information, you can control the people.[51] In a 1529 sermon on Jesus before Pilate, Luther stated:

> We should wash the fur of the magistrate and clean out his mouth whether he laughs or rages. . . . Christ did not say to Pilate, "You have no power over me." He said that Pilate did have power, but he said that, "You do not have this power from yourself. It is given to you from God." Therefore he upbraided Pilate. We do the same. We recognize the authority, but we must rebuke the Pilates in their crime and self-confidence. . . . There is a big difference between suffering injustice and keeping still. The Christian must bear testimony for the truth and die for the truth. But how can he die for the truth if he has not first confessed the truth? Thus Christ showed that Pilate did exercise authority from God and at the same time rebuked him for doing wrong.[52]

Hence the Latin text of the Augsburg Confession begins with the reference to Psalm 119:46, a reference that "most likely comes from Luther's correspondence of the time":[53] "I will also speak of your decrees before kings, and shall not be put to shame."

Here the public activity of ministry is focused on realizing justice and love for the neighbor in the worldly realm. As Luther stated in his 1527–28 "Lectures on I Timothy": "The first moral work of love among Christians is toward civil office."[54] This includes prayer for public officials on behalf of evil men, so that peace may endure. Thus political activity is not an end in itself nor an autonomous temporal pursuit but rather part of God's activity in the world.

Such "unmasking" of injustice and "opening the eyes of secular authorities" is not done in a corner but in the preaching office "in the congregation," "openly and boldly before God and men" (Ps. 82).[55] It is God's will, Luther continues, "that those who are in the office [of ministry] and are called to do so shall rebuke and judge their gods [i.e., the princes] boldly and openly."[56]

> To rebuke rulers is not seditious, provided it is done in the way here described: namely, by the office to which God has committed that duty, and through God's Word, spoken publicly, boldly, and

> honestly. To rebuke rulers in this way is, on the contrary a praiseworthy, noble, and rare virtue, and a particularly great service to God, as the psalm [Psalm 82] here proves. It would be far more seditious if a preacher did not rebuke the sins of rulers; for then he makes people angry and sullen, strengthens the wickedness of the tyrants, becomes a partaker in it, and bears responsibility for it.[57]

"For a preacher is neither a courtier nor a hired hand. He is God's servant and slave, and his commission is over lords and slaves; as the psalm says: 'He judges and rebukes the gods.' . . . He is to do what is right and proper, not with a view to favor or disfavor, but according to law, that is, according to God's Word, which knows no distinction or respect of persons."[58] But, as Luther noted in a sermon on Jesus cleansing the Temple, the civil authorities want to control the pulpit in order to hear only what they approve. The more things change, the more they stay the same: in June 2005, the IRS initiated a case against All Saints Episcopal Church in Pasadena, California, to revoke its tax-exempt status on the basis of an anti-war, anti-poverty sermon preached on the eve of the 2004 election.[59]

To Luther the social ethics of justice and equity are spiritual questions to be addressed by the civil use of laws and regulations designed to restrain greed and promote the common good. Luther's ministry occurred, as they say, in interesting times marked by stark economic disparities, rebellions and wars, plagues and famines, as well as the upheavals of the Reformation. Following his death in 1546, these conditions continued to worsen as wars of religion raged until exhausted in the Thirty Years' War (1618–48). Nevertheless, Luther's vision of the liturgy after the liturgy continued into the modern period, with variations on the theme, through the work of Pietist leaders such as Philipp Jakob Spener and August Hermann Francke and nineteenth-century founders of the modern diaconal movements and Inner Mission, such as Theodor Fliedner and Johann Hinrich Wichern.

For Further Reading

Bayer, Oswald. *Theology the Lutheran Way*. Grand Rapids: Eerdmans, 2007.

Forde, Gerhard. "Radical Lutheranism." *Lutheran Quarterly* 1, no. 1 (1987): 5–18.

Hanawalt, Emily Albu, and Carter Lindberg, eds. *Through the Eye of a Needle: Judeo-Christian Roots of Social Welfare*. Kirksville, Mo.: Thomas Jefferson University Press, 1994.

Lindberg, Carter. *Beyond Charity: Reformation Initiatives for the Poor*. Minneapolis: Fortress Press, 1993.

———. Chapter 5 (on social welfare). In *The European Reformations*. Oxford: Blackwell, 1996.

———. "Luther's Concept of Offering." *Dialog* 35, no. 4 (1996): 251–57.

McKim, Donald K., ed. *The Cambridge Companion to Martin Luther*. Cambridge: Cambridge University Press, 2003.

Rieth, Ricardo. "Luther on Greed." In *Harvesting Martin Luther's Reflections on Theology, Ethics, and the Church*, ed. Timothy J. Wengert, 152–68. Grand Rapids: Eerdmans, 2004.

Torvend, Samuel. *Luther and the Hungry Poor: Gathered Fragments*. Minneapolis: Fortress Press, 2008.

Witte, John, Jr. *Law and Protestantism: The Legal Teachings of the Lutheran Reformation*. Cambridge: Cambridge University Press, 2002.

4

Faith Active in Love

The Development of Modern Lutheran Social Witness

Eric W. Gritsch

Lutheran social witness in Europe after the Reformation is linked to and shaped by two major Lutheran movements: Pietism (1635–1817) and the Confessional Awakening, which was precipitated by the tercentenaries of the Reformation (1517–1817) and the Augsburg Confession (1530–1830). These movements appear in the broad historical context of Romanticism, the industrial revolution of the late eighteenth and nineteenth centuries, and twentieth-century modernity in the wake of the world wars.

The Role of Pietism

Pietism opposed a period of Orthodoxy (1580–1675), which was driven by second-generation German Lutherans who defined the authority of the Word of God as "pure teaching" (*reine Lehre*) communicated by a rationalistic system based on the Bible without much emphasis on personal and social witness.[1] The name "Pietists" appeared in 1675 in a poem: "What is a Pietist? He who on God's Word in his study feeds and then, accordingly, also a holy life leads."[2] The Pietist reform program was launched in Frankfurt am Main by Philipp Jakob Spener (1635–1705) in a manifesto entitled *Pious Desires* (*Pia Desideria*), which proposed six steps of reform in order to overcome the deformation of the church in the wake of Orthodoxy and the Thirty Years' War (1618–48). These steps stressed Bible study in small groups;

a revival of the laity ("common priesthood of all the baptized," as Luther put it); and a less academic, more practical ministry. Personal conversion and commitment to social witness constitute the guiding "desire," namely, that "Christianity should consist more of practice than of knowledge"; the essence of practice is love of neighbor, first among Christians, then toward all people.[3] Such a "practical Christianity" governed the minds of Pietists who desired to launch a second Reformation in the name of Luther in the wake of the devastations of the Thirty Years' War. It was a move from a religion of the mind (Orthodoxy) to a religion of the heart—that is, piety based on inward, spiritual conversion and outward social witness to the gospel.

Among Spener's disciples was August Hermann Francke (1663–1727), a young, vivacious scholar from Saxony leading postwar educational reform programs at the court of Duke Ernest of Saxony-Gotha. He was also a linguist, fluent in major modern European languages, and well trained in ancient Hebrew and Eastern languages as the basis for biblical studies. After an intensive conversion experience in 1687, he used his lectures at Leipzig University with emotional appeals to join Pietist groups devoted to Bible study, prayer, and social action. In order to serve the academy and the church, Francke accepted a call as professor of classical Greek and Eastern languages at the new university in Halle and as pastor to St. George Church in Glaucha near Halle. Within a few years, Francke's preaching and initiatives for social reforms made Halle the hub of the spreading Pietist movement. Orthodox opposition waned and lost its influence. When Francke was called in 1714 as pastor to the large city church of St. Ulrich, he pioneered programs of social ministry that attracted many pastors as well as laypeople and even impressed the Prussian king, Frederick William I (1713–40), who sought ways of dealing with the problems of the postwar years.

Francke began his social ministry with sermons against the abuse of Sunday through heavy drinking, trying to make it again a "holy day." He also put an alms box outside his parsonage. When someone put a larger-than-average sum of money into it, he viewed it as a sign to gather orphaned children in the street for an educational program. Eventually he bought the house next door to the parsonage for use as a boarding school. When more money came in, he converted the building into an orphanage. The young victims of the Thirty Years' War had found a safe home. Since all schools were private, he opened a school. It was the beginning of Francke's career as a social reformer.[4]

Soon there was a school system for students from every walk of life, known as the Halle Foundation. Rich Prussian noble families supported Francke's projects, which soon included a bookstore and a printing press. The rich nobleman, Freiherr Carl Hildebrandt von Canstein, created and headed a Bible institute in 1710, the first in the world, known later as the Canstein Bible Institute and a model for future Bible societies. It printed and distributed two million Bibles in the eighteenth century. It developed into an enduring publication center, printing a variety of works distributed worldwide to this day. A school physician, Christian Richter (1676–1711), founded a pharmaceutical factory with laboratories and supply stores, supported by profits from the sale of new drugs. There was free medical care, and free daily meals were served to students, the poor, and the homeless. More than one hundred university students received free meals and, in turn, often assisted in the programs of teaching and caring for orphans. Francke began to call the Halle Foundation "New Jerusalem" and sent out a series of tracts to anyone he knew at home and abroad: "The Footsteps of the Still Living and Ruling, Loving and Loyal God."

Francke combined his social ministry with a reform of theological education for pastors at the university. Every Thursday morning from ten to eleven he lectured on the relationship of the Bible to Christian life. The university kept this time open in the academic curriculum at Halle University so that all students could attend. Francke concentrated on the interpretation of Paul's pastoral letters, especially 2 Timothy and Titus. Twelve handwritten notes from students are still extant, disclosing the style and content of Francke's lectures. He himself published a distillation of the lectures from 1703 to 1727 in several treatises, with recommendations for the training of pastors according to Spener's ideals that stressed biblical studies, preaching, pastoral care, and commitment to social reform.[5] Two other colleagues joined him in these efforts, resulting in a new Pietist curriculum that focused on biblical studies with practical applications. The three Halle professors attracted students from all over Europe. Among the Halle faculty was Francke's son-in-law, John A. Freylinghausen, who published a popular hymnal in 1704.

The Prussian court used military chaplains trained in Halle and fully supported Francke's efforts as an employee of the government. All schools in the territory were transformed into Halle Foundation schools, the first public school system in Germany. An elitist royal institute, named after King

Frederick (Collegium Fredericianum), educated the best minds of Germany, among them the eminent philosopher Immanuel Kant (1724–1804) and Johann Gottfried Herder (1744–1803), who pioneered a new, nonrationalist view of humanity. But the centerpiece of the Halle Foundation was the education of young children for a good life, based on the well-proven notion that poverty and other social ills must be overcome by an educated mind.

When Francke died in 1727, his "German schools" had instructed 17,500 students, staffed by 4 inspectors and about 100 teachers (including 8 women). The "Latin schools" had 400 students, 3 inspectors, and 32 teachers. A training school for teachers had 82 students, 27 teachers, and 1 inspector.[6] Graduates of the Halle Foundation were to be sent everywhere, realizing Francke's vision: "Transform the world by transforming people." Influential missionaries and church leaders hailed from Halle, among them the patriarch of American Lutheranism, Henry Melchior Muhlenberg (1711–87).

Since Francke was a friend of the court—indeed, enjoyed a cordial relationship with the king—the Halle mission became aligned with the Prussian court, which exhibited the king's military nationalism. The Halle Foundation agreed to create a military orphanage and to publish handbooks for the formation of "Christian soldiers." Thus national political interests diminished the development of independent and ecumenical programs of social ministry.

Francke's son, Gotthilf August Francke (1696–1789), continued the social ministry of the foundation. But he did not have the reputation of his father—a cosmopolitan, charming, bewigged linguist and patriarchal administrator, as well as a pied piper who attracted people of all ages.

The Confessional Awakening Responds to the Industrial Revolution

The nineteenth-century Confessional Awakening in Germany and Scandinavia also focused on social ministry because of the impact of the industrial revolution of the late eighteenth and nineteenth centuries. The new industries brought radical social changes through new technology, such as the steam locomotive, the telegraph, and electric lighting. Moreover, radical ideological changes were proposed by the free market system of Adam Smith, favoring corporate financial power (capitalism), and by the socialism or communism of Karl Marx, calling for a political takeover by workers and labor unions ("the dictatorship of the proletariat").[7] Radical social changes had already been advocated and partially implemented by the Declaration of Independence in the United States in 1776 and the French Revolution in 1789.

In Scandinavia, the Danish pastor Nikolaj F. S. Grundtvig (1783–1872) wove together the Christian tradition with Danish culture through education, worship, and patriotism, though without specific programs of social ministry; unlike Germany, Scandinavia did not experience the devastations of the Thirty Years' War and did not encounter the difficult problems linked to the rebuilding of a suffering society. Another Danish pastor, Vilhelm Beck (1829–1901), combined religious revival with social witness in numerous centers for "home mission." The Swedish pastor Lars Levi Laestadius (1800–1861) and the lay preacher Carl Olof Rosenius (1816–68) called for a general moral regeneration and social reforms in the wake of the industrial revolution. The Finnish farmer Paavo Ruotsalainen (1777–1852), "the prophet of the wilderness," called for individual conversion as the source for social change.[8]

Hans Nielsen Hauge (1771–1824), a lay preacher of the awakening in Norway, focused on a social ministry in the face of radical social changes in Europe. He became inspired by Martin Luther and preached a "living faith" over against the stale spirituality of the Lutheran state church. Since he held assemblies without the approval of the church, he was often in jail, but was finally released in 1811. He married, bought a farm, and founded a number of mills and factories. But he refused to become a "capitalist," giving his profits to others to improve their lives. He also helped to create factories and mills that survived the economic crisis caused by the Napoleonic wars (1800–1815). While greedy timber barons and owners of ironworks went bankrupt, his initiatives and ways of responsible prosperity led to a new rise in Norwegian wealth accompanied by political independence from Denmark in 1814.

Despite his difficulties with the state church, he urged his followers in his last will and testament to remain loyal to the church, thus preserving social ministry in Norwegian Lutheranism.[9] Since 1891 the inner mission movement in Norway was led by a central committee, which directed an increasing number of small associations, clubs, and societies. Because the law against associations outside the church had been revoked in 1841, the success of small local and regional associations shaped social ministry and created a club-like Lutheranism in Norway hardly matched in other countries.[10]

In Germany, the center of the Confessional Awakening, also called "neo-Lutheranism," was the University of Erlangen. One of its graduates, the pastor Wilhelm Löhe (1808–72), accepted a call in 1817 to the small Bavarian town of Neuendettelsau, where he created a model parish of neo-Lutheranism. It was guided by his vision of Christian unity and a wholesome social life. He reformed the liturgy in 1841 and created programs of social ministry, focusing on education and hospital care. In 1841 he founded a mission society to train emergency pastors to care for German emigrants in North America, Australia, and Brazil. Above all, he organized the first deaconess community in 1854 to offer women an opportunity to serve in the church. Löhe wanted to convey to neo-Lutherans the notion that their church should be an ecumenical and social model in a region dominated by conservative Roman Catholicism; he also was instrumental in creating the Lutheran Church–Missouri Synod.[11]

There were other attempts to link the Confessional Awakening with a general concern for the biblical call to love the neighbor. The Lutheran pastor John F. Oberlin (1740–1826) in Waldbach, Alsace, sought social justice by creating savings banks, agricultural societies, and schools for the children of poor families. When another Lutheran pastor, John Falk (1768–1828), encountered homeless orphans, including small children and teenagers, he founded the Society for Friends in Need (*Gesellschaft für Freunde in der Not*) and organized foster homes and "houses of recovery" (*Rettungshäuser*) for juvenile delinquents in Weimar; the best known house was the Luther Court (*Lutherhof*).

The Lutheran pastor in Kaiserswerth (near Düsseldorf), Theodor Fliedner (1800–1864), journeyed to Holland and England to collect funds for his poor parish. In England he encountered the victims of the industrial revolution and the work of the Mennonite diaconate. In 1826, he founded a society for prison reform, which worked with prisoners after their release. He was particularly concerned with the place of women in society. So he founded girls' schools for all ages and institutes to train women teachers. Women were also trained as nurses in a hospital he founded. In a deaconess house he established, women trained to be teachers and professionals in pastoral care as an alternative to ordination, still denied by the church. The house became a model for numerous "mother houses," including one in Pittsburgh and another in Jerusalem. In 1844, Fliedner began to train women as "parish sisters" (*Gemeindeschwestern*), who assisted pastors. His work to increase the role of women in the church made him a "pioneer of the modern women's movement."[12] Fliedner's publishing house in Kaiserswerth produced and distributed many of his tracts and Christian calendars. In 1861, Kaiserswerth employed 380 deaconesses in 26 mother houses, together with 83 satellites abroad. Fliedner also founded a center for the training of deacons and male parish helpers in Duisburg in 1844.

The Beginnings of the Inner Mission Movement

Lutheran social ministry became institutionalized in the Inner Mission movement in Germany and to a lesser degree in Scandinavia. The movement was dedicated to realizing Luther's call for "faith active in love," especially in situations of social need and decay. The emphasis was not only on "foreign mission" but also on "home mission."[13]

The movement was organized in Germany by the Lutheran pastor Johann Hinrich Wichern (1808–81), who was influenced by Luther, Pietism, the Confessional Awakening, and radical political events. The political events were linked to the social changes produced by the industrial revolution, the threat of tyranny—either by a dictatorial Napoleon or by the ideology of Karl Marx—and the "revolution" in the spring of 1848 (street riots in Berlin and other major European cities). Wichern became convinced that human sin is not only spiritual but material, disclosed in an unwholesome division of society, and most obvious in the division between the rich and the poor. He contended that sociopolitical sins had to be confronted with a solid education involving family life, school, and vocational labor within the framework of church and state. The front lines of social action were policies aiming for economic justice, especially in labor practices, taxes, private property, housing, public assistance, and other areas affecting people's well-being. If government was too slow or unwilling to introduce such policies, the Inner Mission would enact reform by enhancing the Christian spiritual formation of individuals called to become missionaries. These representatives of the Inner Mission would renew society through demonstrating their love of neighbor—that is, through service (*diakonia* in Greek).

Wichern envisaged his Inner Mission movement as a key moment in the history of salvation that had begun with Jesus.[14]

While in his pastorate in Hamburg, Wichern encountered teenagers who were in danger of becoming criminals because of poor schools and a lack of parental supervision. Aware of an enterprise known as "houses of recovery" linked to Pastor John Falk in Weimar, in 1833 Wichern used donations to buy and organize a "rough house" (*rauhes Haus*), which offered education, vocational counseling, and training to help other needy people. The inhabitants were called "brethren" (women worked separately as "deaconesses"), and they were trained to work with prisoners, alcoholics, migrants spending nights in hostels, and the homeless.

The rough house became the wellspring of the Lutheran Inner Mission; Wichern adopted this designation from Friedrich Lücke (1791–1855), a disciple of the eminent theologian Friedrich Schleiermacher (1768–1834), and made it popular. It was to be a Christian renewal movement within the church, which had virtually ignored social problems.[15] When a printing press was added to the rough house, Wichern promoted his work at home and abroad through tracts entitled "Flying Leaflets from the Rough House." His popular treatise of 1844, "The State of Distress in the Protestant Church and the Inner Mission," got the attention of the Prussian king, who liked Wichern's program for prisoners and proposed to align his programs of social ministry with royal efforts to make Prussia a "Christian state"—using Wichern's theological ideal as a wedge against godless, secular revolutionaries, specifically Marxists. Numerous "associations" (*Vereine*) sprang up in many locations, especially in the cities, led by graduates of the rough house, who were now known as "fathers of the poor" (*Armenväter*). They trained craftsmen; organized workplaces, shelters, and visits to prisons; and coordinated other diaconical enterprises. Laypeople constituted the majority of volunteers, and the associations used church buildings for meetings.

A visit to associations in Upper Silesia, led by rough house graduates, introduced Wichern to "a major scene of death and tears," and the Berlin street riots in March 1848 motivated him to intensify the Inner Mission by aligning it with antirevolutionary politics. Although a chastened King Frederick William IV (1795–1861) survived the revolution, a conservative political party that had just formed was the major power to preserve the status quo. Wichern supported it as the best way to further "Christian social" ideals.

In 1848 Wichern made national headlines after he gave an emotional, impromptu speech at the first national Church Day (*Kirchentag*) in Wittenberg to a large rank-and-file assembly of Protestants as they deliberated the future work of the church. The speech was an appeal to the state church to adopt the Inner Mission as its special program, armed against social evils and atheistic socialism. The response was a standing ovation. Within the next few weeks the Central Committee for the Inner Mission of the German Protestant Church was organized, consisting of civil servants with noble backgrounds and four theologians. The committee sanctioned the Inner Mission's existing efforts and called for an expansion of programs throughout Germany; new Inner Mission institutions were created in all of the nation's territories. Volunteers were to be trained and supervised by agents from a central office in Hamburg and Berlin. An annual congress of the Inner Mission was held, chaired by the editor of the "Flying Leaflets from the Rough House."

In 1849 Wichern summarized his vision of social ministry in a treatise to the German people, "The Inner Mission of the German Protestant Church." Its leitmotif is the notion of a sporadically unfolding kingdom of God on earth through saving love. Wichern argued that the Inner Mission must be carried out by the organized church and remain within it. It is the work of all members—the clergy and the laity (a "common priesthood")—and its goal is the restoration of responsible individuals who serve God through family, government, and church. Between 1849 and 1857—the Inner Mission added to the associations' work many other projects, such as child care centers, work with prostitutes and alcoholics, lobbying for Sabbath (Sunday) rest, distributing Bibles and Christian tracts, offering pastoral care for sailors and emigrants, and a special "city mission" in Hamburg for those who lived outside the church. This last was a "midnight mission" for prostitutes, prisoners, gypsies, and the homeless and featured preaching in the streets and missions to night clubs. The Inner Mission has learned techniques from the tradition of the city missions founded in Glasgow in 1826 and London in 1835. Eight missionaries would go from house to house, Bible in hand, and talk to unchurched citizens.[16]

In 1856 the church elected Wichern to serve in the Central Council (*Oberkirchenrat*) in Berlin, and the king appointed him to head the Prussian prison system as part of the Department for Domestic Affairs; he also remained pastor at his church. But a stroke in 1866 limited Wichern's numerous activities, and he retired in 1874. The work of the Inner Mission was continued by its Central Committee, which employed 119 "agents" and 88 "correspondents" beginning in 1857.[17]

Around the time of Wichern's retirement, the Inner Mission generated numerous enterprises representing a mixture of associations, institutions, and other general efforts to create a civil and moral environment through Sabbath laws, Sunday schools, and publications. Special efforts were made to care for soldiers in the various military campaigns of the nineteenth century. In the late nineteenth century, the Inner Mission joined other social ministry efforts, such as the international Blue Cross *(Blaues Kreuz)* in 1877, which was headquartered in Geneva and treated alcoholism and other addictions; the Young Men's Christian Association in 1889; and the Committee of Mission to German Sailors in 1895. But the creative spirit of Wichern and the zeal of his followers waned, and the church could not be motivated to instill a Christian social spirit in the rising labor movement. Secular socialism determined its future.

Bodelschwingh and the Inner Mission

In 1872, the Inner Mission received new leadership in the dynamic nobleman Friedrich von Bodelschwingh (1831–1910).[18] On his Westphalian estate near Tecklenburg he became acquainted with the Confessional Awakening and read tracts published by the Inner Mission. He decided to study theology in Basel, Switzerland, and become a missionary. He was impressed by the work of Wilhelm Löhe and by the healing ministry of Pastor John C. Blumhardt in Bad Boll.[19] But when he finished his studies, doubts threatened to destroy his missionary commitment. A call from the Lutheran church in Paris to care for German immigrants who worked as rag pickers and street sweepers restored his faith. Using his talents for leading and organizing, Bodelschwingh created a small parish in a poor district, with an elementary school, a parsonage, and a home for teachers. In 1861 he returned home, married, took a parish, and served as military chaplain in the German-French war of 1870–71. Then tragedy struck: within two weeks his four children died during an epidemic of whooping cough. Bodelschwingh confessed later that he had experienced mercy by encountering a hard God.

In 1872, he was asked to head the Westphalian Institute for epileptics and its deaconess house in Bielefeld. A year later, he united all social ministry programs in a new building, calling it Bethel, which was soon to be known worldwide as "the city of mercy." In 1877 Bodelschwingh added a center of brethren (male deacons), naming it Nazareth; he viewed these biblical designations as modern images of the history of salvation through social ministry. In 1882 a center for the "Brethren from the Highway" was added, along with a "work camp" (*Arbeitskolonie*) that trained migrant workers for steady jobs, and in 1903 Bodelschwingh lobbied successfully at the Prussian Diet for a fair labor law for migrant workers. Preventive measures against unemployment were to be taken by a "laborer home" (*Arbeiterheim*) in 1885 for factory workers. When Bodelschwingh discovered the devastating misery caused by unemployment in Berlin, he created three more centers there in 1905.

Although he cooperated with the government, Bodelschwingh did not share Wichern's ideal of a "Christian state." Aware of the penultimate nature of the Christian life, an interim between the first and second advent of Christ, he knew that all efforts of social ministry only pave the way for a future, eternal kingdom of God. That is why Bodelschwingh did not succumb to the lure of Prussian politics, nor did he measure his work by earthly success; he assumed in his biblical faith that everyone, whether curable or not, is always a child of God destined for the eternal future promised by the gospel. Hope, not obligation, must propel care for others. Here Bodelschwingh made his own distinction between law and gospel. Although traditional Lutheran theology generally views the main function of the law as pedagogical (after creating order it teaches penance and moves sinners to the gospel), he made education for mercy look like a cheerleader for the gospel. As he put it, "force creates anger, but voluntariness creates cheerful people."[20] When he founded a school of theology in Bethel (*theologische Hochschule*) in 1888, he told future pastors that they would be best prepared for their calling by work with a "blue apron" (*blaue Schürze*), the symbol of practical, often manual, labor. Their professors were to be the sick and needy. Thus theological education was, for the first time in Germany, tied to training in the institutes of the Inner Mission.

Bodelschwingh linked the Inner Mission at home with the mission abroad. He founded the Mission Society for East Africa (today Tanzania), headquartered in Bethel and later known as the Bethel Mission Society. The Society added other missions to Africa and created missions for German emigrants in Russia and Brazil. Bodelschwingh had become known as an ingenious beggar who could raise money when no one else could. Known as "Father Bodelschwingh," he was a brilliant organizer with an instinctive sense for programs and their link to institutions and finances. He lived and died with the conviction that no one lives outside the mercy of God. His favorite biblical saying, inscribed on his tombstone, proclaimed, "Since it is by God's mercy that we are engaged in this ministry we do not lose heart" (2 Cor. 4:1).

Bodelschwingh's youngest son, Frederick Jr. (1877–1946), continued the work of his father, who had asked for his assistance with the work at Bethel beginning in 1901. For three decades he directed and expanded the work of his father. New institutions were founded. Above all, the pedagogical arm of the Inner Mission was strengthened through a girls' school for higher learning (*Gymnasium*). Medical care was expanded; Bethel became the world's center for the treatment of epilepsy. For the first time, theology and medicine were united in experiments using spiritual, psychological, and physical therapy for the unemployed and the sick, with the assumption that all clients and patients were part of a mission congregation destined for the kingdom of God. Frederick Jr. was a fascinating preacher and storyteller who could communicate with epileptics when others failed. His sermons and stories were widely read in the "Bethel Messenger." World War I generated a need for massive programs for soldiers on all battlefields, ranging from care for the wounded to providing consoling tracts. In addition, there was social ministry for prisoners and refugees.

During the Weimar Republic (1919–33), Frederick Jr. used the Inner Mission to influence social legislation for welfare and against disenfranchisement. When the regime of Adolf Hitler introduced a euthanasia program for epileptics and others, because they were labeled as "unworthy for life" (*lebensunwert*), Frederick Jr. saved every epileptic in Bethel through his unbending resistance and lobbied successfully for the ending of the program. He and Bethel managed to survive World War II, and his nephew Frederick and the pastor Rudolf Hardt led Bethel into the modern era.

After World War II, the Inner Mission developed programs to assist in the rebuilding of Germany, concentrating on missions for people seeking shelter in railroad stations and for youth, as well as old age homes. In

1945 the Inner Mission created a center for "Protestant relief work" (*evangelisches Hilfswerk*) sanctioned by the government. In 1948 the Evangelical Church in Germany declared that "diaconal-missionary work belongs to the essence and life of the church."[21] In 1957 the Inner Mission became part of the state church and was known as Inner Mission and Relief Work of the Protestant Church in Germany. Its work was carried out by special teams consisting of deacons and deaconesses, educational experts, youth workers, health care professionals, social workers, and other experts. By 1959 there were 107 mother houses with almost 40,000 sisters; centers for deacons with about 4,300 brothers; 3,600 social, educational, and health care institutions; 4,000 nursery schools for 300,000 children; and more than 5,000 centers for general social ministry located in parishes, staffed with nurses and social workers.

The Legacy of Reformation-Era Social Ministry

The major voice of Romanticist philosophy, Johann Gottfried Herder (1744–1803), argued for an affinity between Lutheran social witness and Romanticism, with its emphasis on "light, life, and love."[22] As Lutheran superintendent (later called "bishop") in Weimar, Herder was concerned with leading minds away from the rationalism of the European Enlightenment toward a focus on human feelings and morality based on the example of Jesus and guided by religion as the best part of humanity. This morality was to shape the beginning of an ideal community, exemplified in the world by an "association" that issued new moral power; the church was such an association, and social witness belonged to it. Richard Rothe (1799–1867), a Lutheran professor of ethics in Bonn and Heidelberg, contended that the church should lead all moral associations to become a final "community" (*Gemeinschaft*), reflecting the intentions of Christ, the Savior. According to Rothe, social witness was not a special Christian enterprise but constituted the essence of the church as the model of a civil, moral society committed to justice for all. Rothe even contended that the church should transfer its original obligation to be the principal organ of Christ's historical activity to the state in order to create the final moral community.[23]

This Romanticist view did not have its way in Lutheranism. The court chaplain Adolf Stoecker (1835–1909) successfully opposed the efforts of

Wichern, Rothe, and others to create a Christian state. A sworn enemy of Marxism, he opted for the power of an anti-Socialist political party instead of supporting the political goal of the Inner Mission. He founded the Christian Socialist Labor Party in 1878 with the support of the prominent economist Adolf Wagner (1835–1917), who favored patriarchal charity programs for social ministry rather than any change in the existing social order. Stoecker also founded the Evangelical (Protestant) Congress in 1890, attracting the Prussian intellectual elite. When another Lutheran pastor in Frankfurt, Frederick Naumann (1860–1919), again tried to revive Wichern's vision of a Christian state in the parliament, lobbying for better wages for the working class, Stoecker countered by founding the Free Ecclesiastical-Social Conference in 1897; its members were right-wing members of the Lutheran state church opposed to any compromise. In the end, Stoecker lost all support when he succumbed to anti-Semitism, blaming Jews for the social problems of the day.[24]

In the centuries after the Reformation, men with vision, organizational talents, and stamina developed creative, indeed revolutionary Lutheran social ministry programs. Some of them, like Johann Wichern, tried to realize the ideal of a Christian state with social justice for all. Others, like Hans Nielsen Hauge, were business entrepreneurs and linked Christian faith with fair trade. Social ministry also revealed the church's apathy in the face of radical social change. Nevertheless, in the large state churches of Germany and Scandinavia the Inner Mission became an integral part of church policy and joined the efforts of the state to create social justice. In this sense, the Lutheran eucharistic doctrine of the "real presence" found its counterpart in the obedience to the injunction of Jesus: "Truly I tell you, just as you did it to one of the least of these who are members of my family, you did it to me" (Matt. 25:40).

For Further Reading

Arden, G. Everett. *Four Northern Lights: Men Who Shaped Scandinavian Churches*. Minneapolis: Augsburg Publishing House, 1964.

Bradfield, Margaret. *The Great Samaritan: The Life and Work of Friedrich von Bodelschwingh*. London: Marshall, Morgan & Scott, 1964.

Spener, Philip Jacob. *Pia Desideria.* Ed. and trans. Theodore G. Tappert. Philadelphia: Fortress Press, 1964.

Wentz, Abdel R. *Fliedner the Faithful.* Philadelphia: Board of Publications of the Lutheran Church in America, 1936.

5

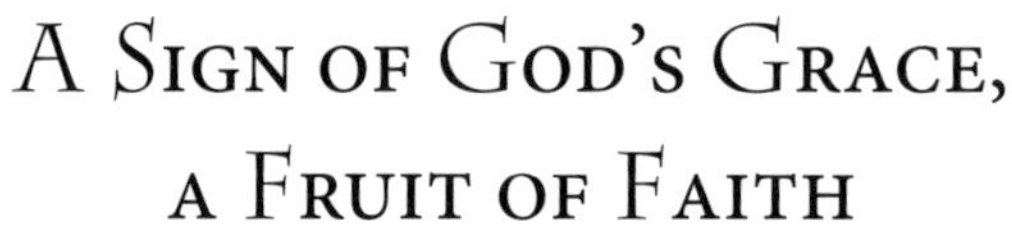

A Sign of God's Grace, a Fruit of Faith

American Lutheran Social Service from 1800 to 1945

Carl T. Uehling

Learning from Our Past

Most Americans are reluctant to discard our dim and distant past, judging by the plethora of historical volumes being published—many fictional but some relatively accurate. Notice, as well, the curiosity engendered by genealogical findings, some gratifying and some mortifying, and the penchant in many quarters for personal museums of bric-a-brac ranging from elderly pennies to Model T Fords! We learn from what has gone before, it is said. Those who ignore their history are condemned to repeat its mistakes. Our children's children must know their heritage.

But we are, of course, radically different from our past. There are many more of us now, so we encounter many more automobiles on many more highways, and many more houses in our neighborhoods and many more rules and regulations trying our patience. We also have many more unsolicited catalogs in our mail, many more gadgets in our homes, many more patients in the waiting rooms of our doctors' offices, as well as many more poisonous pollutants in the air we breathe and the food we eat and the water we drink.

These changes in contemporary society suggest dichotomies. We honor and cherish our great grandparents and grandparents and parents, but we live in the present and for the future. Our forebears may have had simple uncluttered lives, but our lives are complex and complicated. Once upon a time people had commonly accepted principles and expectations defining their roles in their homes and in their communities, but now some fear that almost anything goes and the old taboos are themselves taboo!

This chapter focuses on Lutheran social ministry structures in the United States from 1800 to 1945. Many, if not most, readers likely have no sense of what life was like before 1945 because they were born after that year. Those arriving before that year, by at least a decade or so, remember a fair amount of what that was like, and do so fondly and wistfully, as if everything indeed was preferable in the good old days, even though they know better. Probably their parents were the prime messengers, parents who had experienced firsthand the world wars of the century, the disastrous if unexpected consequences of Prohibition, the suffering and uncertainty of the Depression. Almost miraculously, most got through these and all the other troubles of their times, but not without pain and suffering.

Immigrants and the Churches

The basic premise of this chapter is that church-related institutions, like the churches themselves and the ordinary folks who fill their pews, are very much influenced by the circumstances of their times—social ministry organizations (SMOs) especially. They may credit capable leadership and determined supporters and innovative programs with their effectiveness, but it is society itself that sets their agendas.

Consider, for example, the nation's population growth in the first half of the nineteenth century. Five million citizens in 1800 had swelled to twenty-three million in 1850, primarily because of immigration from Europe. Many of the newcomers were from countries with significant numbers of Lutherans—they were Germans, Swedes, Norwegians, Finns, Danes, Hungarians, Slovaks, and they were enough to total some six hundred thousand souls by the start of the Civil War. Most were escaping their homelands, leaving their families behind, and risking their lives on a perilous and extended journey to what some thought would be a land of milk and honey.

But they did not know the language, their new neighbors were not always hospitable, and they missed life as they had known it back home.

Consequently, they did what people always do in new and strange environments: they sought out places where the neighbors spoke their language and they could worship in their mother tongues.

While the immigrants included a few senior citizens, most were young mainly because of the circumstances surrounding their leaving of their home countries. In Germany an abortive revolution in 1849–50 drove thousands of liberal students and academics into exile, and most ended up in the United States.[1] Moreover, some ancient customs decreed that only the oldest son could inherit the farm, so subsequent children needed to find a new place to raise their families. America, with its cheap land, seemed attractive. Passage to the new country required crossing the Atlantic Ocean in a crowded sailing vessel, and passengers without sufficient stamina were few. Only the young and vigorous could survive the journey.

The Lutheran churches the immigrants encountered in America in the 1800s were hard-pressed to handle the throngs of potential new members. At the time, most church members were the children or grandchildren of immigrants who arrived in the 1700s. These descendants of immigrants were native-born Americans. They spoke English and emulated their Presbyterian and Methodist friends. Their church buildings had little ornamentation and center pulpits. Like other Protestants, they had revival meetings and vigorous preaching but hardly any liturgy, and candles on the communion table were purely functional, to be lit only when required for reading, never when there was plenty of sunlight streaming through the clear glass windows.

The newcomers were dismayed by the practices of what they considered the so-called Lutherans of America. Moreover, old European animosities tended to prevail among them, so Swedes looked for other Swedes, Germans other Germans. Theological issues also had an impact, and the result was chaotic. At one time or another, Lutherans in America had some 250 different synods and denominations.

ABANDONED CHILDREN

Living conditions for immigrants could be dismal, especially when compared to current lifestyles. Housing was crude and less than sanitary, and people were often ill. Average life expectancy in 1800 was thirty-five; by the end of the century it had only reached forty-seven. Some families had as many as a dozen children, but few grew to adulthood. With life spans so constricted, orphaned children were common, and when relatives or neighbors lacked the resources to care for them, those children were prematurely on their own.

Orphanages first appeared in America in 1729, founded by Catholic nuns after an attack by Native Americans killed off adult settlers in Mississippi. By the nineteenth century massive immigration had swelled city populations, and great numbers of orphaned children wandered the streets struggling to stay alive. Many became petty criminals, to the dismay of the citizenry. Facilities created for their care were more for the protection of society than for the welfare of the orphans. One historian has noted that "the orphanage movement begins at just the same time we begin building prisons and state hospitals for the insane. They're all part of the same phenomenon."[2]

Frequently hundreds of children slept row on row in orphanage dormitories. An immense bathtub could hold fifteen or twenty children at a time. Meals were sparse, as was evident from the small stature of those who left when they reached the legal age of fourteen. Staff inflicted harsh punishments for breaking the institution's rules, and children worked long hours in the orphanage's shops and farm fields. In some instances, according to a state investigator, the children were "forced to do drudgery, working eight or nine hours a day, with only one hour for schooling, and that often at night."

Some of the earliest Lutheran social ministry efforts were orphanages, providing housing and care for Lutheran children whose parents had died. Then, when it began to be apparent that adult immigrants were growing older, church members became concerned for their care as well. Aged farmers and laborers had no pensions, no Social Security checks. They had to depend on family or neighbors for support, and when that failed, their only alternative was the county poor farm.

Caring for Their Own

Lutheran pastors and laypeople sometimes took impoverished members into their own homes, and as the numbers of those needing help increased, congregations established facilities devoted to their care. In much the same way, in the aftermath of the Civil War, homes were built for children orphaned by that conflict, as well as to meet the needs of the injured and incapacitated.

New social ministry organizations, while including "Lutheran" in their names, tended not to have been created by Lutheran denominations. But the church bodies themselves were struggling with the continuing flood of immigrants, sending out missionaries to gather them into new congregations, dealing with the problems surfacing because of rapid growth, and trying to preserve their ethnic culture. Social ministry was considered an "inner mission," defined as the charitable work of individual Christians and only obliquely the responsibility of a synod or denomination.

Nor were the SMOs designed to provide care for everyone. Their leaders were not social activists: They did not address the high death rate among newly arrived immigrants that made so many of their children orphans. They did not seek to place responsibility for the care of orphaned children or impoverished old people into the hands of the government. The immigrants, as well as their pastors, had come from European countries in which citizens were expected to obey their rulers without question. They had been taught that God had ordained some to be the kings and rulers and others to be their obedient servants. Americans whose ancestors had fought the "ordained authorities" in the War for Independence now were the ordained authorities themselves. More recent immigrants knew better than to complain.

In 1912 the Federal Council of Churches, representing the major Protestant denominations, adopted a Social Creed of the Churches. It declared that the teachings of Jesus applied to business ethics, organized labor, and social justice. Lutheran leaders ignored it, and most Lutherans were not aware of its existence.[3]

LUTHERAN SOCIAL ACTIVISTS

There were exceptions to Lutheran reticence, however. Abolitionists, in 1837, founded the Franckean Synod because they were opposed to the "great national and heinous sin" of slavery.[4] Samuel Simon Schmucker, the founder of the Lutheran Seminary at Gettysburg, had his library looted by Confederate troops who resented his known support for emancipation. One of Schmucker's students, William Passavant, helped establish hospitals in Illinois, Pennsylvania, and Wisconsin, as well as orphanages in Pennsylvania, New York, and Massachusetts.

In Germany Johann Hinrich Wichern, a layman who had had theological training, established a rescue facility for delinquent boys. He coined the term "inner missions" (in contrast to "foreign" missions) as he called for Christians to have a new emphasis within society. "As the whole Christ reveals himself in the living Word of God," he wrote, "so must Christ proclaim himself in the deeds of God. And the highest, purest, mostly churchly of these actions is saving love."[5]

In America, casework services began in Minnesota, and some orphaned children were placed in foster homes rather than institutions. A family service agency was established in Philadelphia. In the larger cities, because young people were leaving the farms and finding urban employment, hospices were started to serve as "homes away from home." Settlement houses were established in several cities to help the poor through food distribution programs, job training, and counseling.

Tuberculosis, at that time the third highest cause of death in the United States and primarily a disease of the young, prompted the start of a sanatorium in Colorado. One of the larger Lutheran denominations raised money for tents where the sick lived year-round, because it was commonly believed that the cure for the disease required plenty of fresh air. Deaconesses opened a treatment center for tuberculosis victims in Philadelphia; its Board of Managers was composed exclusively of women until the 1950s. On June 15, 1904, St. Mark's Lutheran Church in New York City chartered an excursion boat, and over 1,300 passengers, mostly women and children, boarded the *General Slocum* for a day of relaxation and fresh air. Fire broke out midmorning, and before the horror was over, 1,021 people had died. The congregation never recovered from the loss.

American Lutherans and World War I

But ultimately World War I changed the status quo for everyone. Between 1900 and 1914, American manufacturing output had nearly doubled. Two million people belonged to the American Federation of Labor. Henry Ford was manufacturing 125,000 cars a year. Farmers were enjoying a new era of prosperity, receiving twice as much for their harvests as in the previous decade. The empire-building programs that had been attracting the nations of Europe for decades continued to fill their treasuries with riches from the labor and resources of their colonies. It was "the white man's burden," said the imperialists, to take charge of underdeveloped countries so they could bestow the benefits of Western leadership. Paradoxically, they also declared the superiority of Anglo-European genetics and the "rights" those genetics granted. America flexed its muscles, sending the White Fleet around the world, opening the Panama Canal and policing Central and South America. Ominously, Germany was growing increasingly militaristic. Its emperor wanted "a place in the sun" for the German people, but there was little room left for any new colonies.

When the start of the war, American Lutherans, especially German-speaking Lutherans, were ambivalent about the possibility that the United States would be a party to the European conflict. Prominent church leaders defended Germany. At a synod meeting in 1914 the delegates prayed for Germany and sang "Deutschland über Alles" and "Die Wacht am Rhein." A Lutheran denominational periodical asserted that the war was "the result of the British plan of destroying Germany's foreign commerce and relations."[6] An organization calling itself the American Neutrality League drew the support of German Lutheran newsletters.

Then, when America declared war on Germany in 1917, any Lutheran who spoke with a German accent was suspect.[7] Librarians pulled German language books off their shelves and burned them. German was no longer taught in high schools; Lutheran parochial schools were closed, and some were burned. In a few instances, pastors and church councilmen were tarred and feathered. No wonder, coping with such an outpouring of hostility and prejudice, Lutherans sought to defend each other. Now supporting the war effort, proportionately more Lutherans enlisted than any other religious group.

LUTHERANS UNITED

The Lutheran Commission for Soldiers' and Sailors' Welfare was formed by the various Lutheran denominations, and it sought to help military recruits. Within a year it had changed its name to the National Lutheran Council, uniting eleven church bodies in a loose federation so that Lutherans would have a united voice when addressing American society and the government in Washington. Ironically it was because of the war that Lutherans began to lose some of their provincialism; the walls they had erected between each other and between them and their non-Lutheran neighbors began to disintegrate.

The war also accelerated the Americanization of immigrants and their children. Youngsters who had grown up speaking Swedish or German now practiced their English, though the accents usually remained for another generation or two. Surnames were modified, so "Schmidt" became "Smith" for many, "Becker" became "Baker," and "Zimmerman" became "Carpenter." Parents hesitated to teach their children their native tongue lest they be thought not fully American. After sending their sons off to fight the nation's battles, and after hearing returned veterans describe what it felt like to serve alongside all creeds and nationalities and races, immigrants were more tolerant of their melting-pot society.

It would take another even more destructive war to complete this process of embracing the whole of American life. Incredibly, most Lutheran social ministry organizations in 1950 still confined their services to Lutherans, as a matter of policy. They were being financially supported by Lutheran church members and believed they had an obligation to continue to care only for their own. Yet a few organizations were increasingly serving people who had no direct ties to the Lutheran churches, under the premise that human care was not to be denied because the recipients had not been baptized or confirmed as Lutherans. Those SMOs moved much more quickly into the mainstream of America.

Sadly, though American troops turned the tide in Europe and effectively won the war, we lost the peace.[8] President Woodrow Wilson's effort to secure American participation in the newly formed League of Nations failed in 1920 as a wave of isolationism swept the country. Under a slogan of "America First," international trade and finance policies were inaugurated by Congress that set the stage for the Great Depression and Adolf Hitler's rise to power in Germany.

The Good Life

Life for many Americans in the 1920s was giddy and breathless as the good mixed with the bad in society. In 1919 prohibitionists finally won the adoption of the Eighteenth Amendment. Legislating personal behavior, the amendment declared alcoholic beverages to be illegal. As a result millions of Americans became lawbreakers, and gangster empires made booze their business. "Flappers" in New York and Chicago and Los Angeles bobbed their hair, shortened their skirts, painted their lips, drank and smoked in public, and danced the Charleston all night long.

For years women had been struggling for the right to vote. That victory was largely due to the efforts of Susan B. Anthony, who devoted her life to women's suffrage.[9] At last, in 1920, fourteen years after Anthony's death, the Nineteenth Amendment was ratified, giving women that right. But it would still be decades before many women would head major corporations or win political contests or become ordained Lutheran pastors.

Half a million African Americans had moved north for wartime jobs during the war. Now returned white veterans competed with them for jobs, and race riots left their scars on northern cities. The Ku Klux Klan reawakened and gained considerable strength in the North, South, and Midwest by violently targeting African Americans and Roman Catholics. Phalanxes of hooded "knights" confronted Protestant pastors during Sunday services, ostentatiously parading forward with monetary gifts that the intimidated clergy usually accepted. Acceptance meant tacit approval, but then, most white Americans, clergy included, believed that black people, whose grandparents had been slaves, should "know their place."

More and more automobiles were on the road. Newspaper headlines hinted at lurid tales of sex and scandal. At the start of the 1920s regular licensed radio broadcasts inaugurated what would eventually become a mammoth entertainment industry. John T. Scopes was found guilty of teaching evolution to his high school students in Dayton, Tennessee, and fined $100 and costs, but in reality evolution science was the big winner in its struggle against "superstition." Charles A. Lindbergh flew nonstop from New York to Paris, traveling 3,610 miles in thirty-three and a half hours. The next year Amelia Earhart became the first woman to fly over the Atlantic Ocean.

It was a prosperous time for American businesses. Only 3.2 percent of employable workers were unemployed in 1925, with many people working in the bustling textile, pharmaceutical and technology, and construction and transportation industries. Farm kids pestered their parents till they relented and allowed their offspring to seek their fortunes in the city. Thus the youngsters escaped the slower pace of the countryside, but very few found great success.

In Germany, the economy was in tatters. Inflation and unemployment skyrocketed. By 1923 the price of a single loaf of bread had risen to a million marks. Authorities took to stamping newly printed bills with larger denominations, but that didn't help. Some people burned paper money just to keep warm. Those hoping to escape to America could not afford the tariff. Only people with rich relatives in the States could make the journey, providing their kin sent the necessary funds.

The fledgling National Lutheran Council, in the aftermath of the armistice, made it possible for the various Lutheran denominations in America to participate in sending clothing, food, and money (almost $8 million in ten years) to the war-ravaged churches of Europe. Still more assistance was sent to a million starving German-speaking Lutherans in Russia. Unfortunately, these inter-Lutheran efforts raised certain tensions among the more conservative Lutheran groups who opposed any kind of aid to overseas churches that they considered to be too theologically liberal. Clearly issues concerning cultural values and theological viewpoints, in addition to linguistic differences, still separated American Lutherans. Many of the Lutherans who had overwhelmed the Lutheran landscape after the Civil War as yet had no intentions of disappearing into America's melting pot, and they were determined to preserve their religious and cultural heritage.

The leaders of Lutheran SMO were fully aware of the arguments among the separate church bodies, but they were more onlookers than active participants. Many had reached out to each other with counsel and advice, and joint efforts between independent SMOs were underway in several cities. Two national social welfare confederations were started in 1922, the Lutheran Welfare Conference and the Lutheran Inner Mission Conference. These groups enabled like-minded people from all Lutheran denominations to join in efforts addressing the common good.

The boisterous economy of the 1920s provided a variety of funding for building projects all over the SMO landscape. Plans for these improvements had been postponed during the war. But now remodeling projects and additions to existing structures increased the space required for guests and also improved services to them. About 10 percent of present-day SMOs can trace their beginnings to the period between 1920 and 1939, a proportion that likely would have been much higher if the Depression had not intervened.

It is also apparent that agencies committed to serving those with specific problems could adjust when circumstances changed for their charges, suggesting that their motivation, overall, was not so much the meeting of a given need as it was their devotion to the care of people without exception. When the incidence of tuberculosis declined, some of the sanitariums closed their doors, but some were converted to other uses. Increasingly people who engaged in social work were better educated; and the disciplines they were taught, and their enthusiasm for their work, began to influence the nature of the programs being offered, especially in facilities serving children. Alternatives they suggested included foster care, moving away from institutions, and possibilities for new areas of service, particularly geriatrics.

CHANGES IN THE CHURCHES

Meanwhile, the character of Lutheran churches whose members supported the work of local SMOs was changing. In 1920 two-thirds of all the sermons preached in the pulpits of the Norwegian Lutheran Church in America were in the Norwegian language. Ten years later two-thirds of the sermons were in English, and use of the mother tongue was rapidly diminishing. The same children who were abandoning their parents' languages were also fleeing the family farms to live and work in the cities. When they married, it was to mates from other distant places, and often to non-Lutherans. New ethnic flavoring was added to the Lutheran stew by these strangers the old folks sought to accept and love.

In the 1920s 1,500 new Lutheran congregations were founded, a gain of almost 20 percent. By 1930 there were 16,532 Lutheran congregations in America.[10] New York City and its suburbs had 540 Lutheran churches. Mushrooming growth was also occurring in other cities, as well as in Sunbelt states like California and Florida. The robust health of inner mission organizations reflected the robust health of the churches, although, for the most part, their services continued much as before with residential care for the aged and for orphans.

Almost 800,000 Americans were killed or wounded in the Civil War, while the toll for our participation in the first World War was about 320,000.

Thus the effect of the latter war on the lives of American children was proportionately lower. By that time, also, the care given to orphaned children was much improved. Orphanages tended to consist of sturdy structures surrounded by plowed fields and vegetable gardens. The children ate food they had helped plant, tend, and harvest. They were educated in their own schools and wore orphanage uniforms (or hand-me-down clothing from local church members). In the larger institutions youngsters were prepared for adult life as mechanics, farmers, carpenters, printers, seamstresses, or secretaries.

Social ministry leaders were proud of their orphanages, more so than their homes for the aging. The latter were often dreary institutions, redolent of bodily wastes and staffed, largely, by poorly trained and overworked attendants who often had little patience or compassion for their charges. But the orphanages were different, the crowning jewels in the SMO tiaras. Children, especially small children, evoked pity, smiles, concern, and, truth be told, financial support. A choir or orchestra of winsome, well-behaved children appearing before local congregations always left audiences tearful and offering plates overflowing. Few could resist an appeal for funds to support the orphans. A few social ministry leaders questioned the orphanage concept, suggesting that carefully chosen foster homes were better for children than institutions, but it would take a national Depression to force a change.

The Effects of the Great Depression

There were plenty of signs of economic weakness as the decade of the '20s came to a close, but expert analysts still cannot agree on a precise cause for the stock market crash on October 29, 1929. Those who played the market lost an estimated $50 billion in a single day. Large corporations were wiped out. Unemployment soared from 3.2 percent in 1929 to 24.9 percent in 1933. People lost their jobs and then, unable to pay their mortgages, lost their homes. Child malnutrition rates rose to dangerous levels. Families broke up, angry marital partners blaming each other for what was beyond their control. People did without adequate medical care, hoping for the best. It was not until the nation was fully involved in World War II that unemployment was lowered to pre-crash levels. And inasmuch as other nations of the world depended on America's economic well-being, everyone everywhere ran out of economic steam. Suffering was far worse overseas than in the United States.

Responding to the crisis, President Franklin D. Roosevelt issued a series of decrees and programs. Under his leadership, Congress passed the New Deal in 1933, with measures to regulate banks, distribute funds to the unemployed, create jobs, raise agricultural prices, and set wage and production standards for industry. The Works Progress Administration (WPA), instituted in 1935, employed millions of people and affected almost every locality, building many public buildings and roads and operating large arts, drama, media, and literacy projects. It also fed children and distributed food, clothing, and housing. The WPA was closed by Congress because of the war boom in 1943, but another Depression creation is still with us: Social Security, also started in 1935, initially provided pensions, unemployment insurance, and help for the poor.

Thus began, in the Great Depression of the 1930s, the ultimate reversal of roles between SMOs and the government. Simply put, the SMOs had never had, and would never have, resources sufficient to deal with the issues created by such severe economic distress. Government had always had the responsibility to provide protection to its citizens in the event of attacks from foreign invaders or loss from criminally inclined members of American society. Now, in response to adverse economic conditions never before encountered in the nation's history, it assumed responsibility for those suffering from natural calamities, social forces, physical disabilities, or the aging process. No amount of essentially private philanthropy would come close to meeting the level of desperate need.

This was especially true because the providers of that largesse were themselves also the victims of hard times. The human flood that had watered the incredible growth of the Lutheran church bodies in America slowed to a mere trickle as immigration fell by 88 percent. Congregations had to find ways to survive with less money and fewer members. Building plans were cancelled. Pastors went without salaries, surviving, if they could, only by the generosity of members with large vegetable gardens. Church basements were given over to impoverished families who had lost their homes.

The SMOs' Struggle to Survive

Social ministry organizations also found themselves struggling to stay alive. Human nature being what it is, church members tend to give first to their congregation, then to other benevolent causes. When resources grow scarce, most people cut back much more on their giving to people they do not even know. The ultimate consequences were drastic for those at the end of the chain, the aged guests who did not have enough resources to cover the cost of their care, even as the institutions where they lived were exhausting whatever small cash reserves they had accumulated through diligent management.

One home for the aging recalled this anxious period about fifty years later. "The question in the minds of the Board members and friends," they wrote, "was not whether the home would survive, but how." They organized aid societies in their supporting churches to raise funds, collect clothing, and provide Christmas gifts for residents. Board members sometimes emptied their own pockets to meet payrolls or other financial emergencies and often gave of their time to perform maintenance. Their reminiscence concluded that "the twenty years following the Depression were the worst of times for the Home financially; yet, they may have been the best of times. Out of the struggle for survival emerged a remarkable unity among supporters and staff, a clear sense of purpose and a vision for the future."

Many social ministry leaders were advocating greater inter-Lutheran cooperation. The pace of realignment, mergers, and restructuring accelerated, even though some facilities were forced to close (temporarily or permanently) as a result of fiscal difficulties. It was also true, however, that in those tough times concerned people did come together so as to keep programs alive, and that under the strains imposed by such adversities the universal need to meet payrolls could take priority over any doctrinal disagreements.

Another lesson about cooperation was learned from a different segment of the Lutheran witness in America. The National Lutheran Council in 1934 assumed responsibility for recruiting Lutheran pastors to serve as military chaplains. It also acted as a liaison between the chaplains and their churches. About the same time the Lutheran Church–Missouri Synod began its Army and Navy Commission to function in a similar manner.

Both negotiated directly with the military's chief of chaplains, underscoring the need for a united front when addressing society and its governmental authorities.

America during World War II

Most of the news, in the 1930s, was bad news. Shortly after Hitler was named chancellor in 1933, opposition parties were disbanded, strikes were outlawed, and all economic, cultural, and religious life was brought under the control of the Nazi Party. That same year, the concentration camp at Dachau was opened, and thousands of Jews were killed. Yet unemployment was ended, and many German immigrants in America praised Hitler and his cohorts for freeing the homeland from the shame of the 1918 defeat. Italy overran Ethiopia, Japan invaded China, and in Spain a civil war left a million dead and the country under the control of the extreme right. Also, in America in 1933, Prohibition was adjudged to be a mistake, and the Twenty-First Amendment of the nation's Constitution restored the right to drink alcoholic beverages to the citizenry. Germany's spectacular dirigible, the Hindenburg, exploded while landing in 1937. Orson Welles broadcast a radio dramatization depicting an invasion from Mars in 1938, and thousands of frightened listeners clogged New Jersey roads trying to escape the visitors from outer space. But the specter looming over all the world was that of Adolf Hitler as he flaunted the resurgent military might of Germany.

The Second World War began on September 1, 1939, when Germany declared war on Poland after signing a nonaggression pact with the Soviet Union the month before. The century that had begun with such promise had already endured almost ten million deaths in a global conflict, dozens of smaller skirmishes, and a devastating depression. Now, when everyone thought it could not get worse, it became worse than anyone could imagine.

As with any other time in human history, changes came slowly, and pain and suffering were ameliorated by seasons of relief and joy. In the 1930s typical American families heated their houses with coal and refrigerated their food with an icebox, but they seldom complained. If they forgot to empty the pan collecting melted ice water they had a flooded pantry, so they tried not to forget. They might not have had a telephone, but they could have a radio shaped like an airplane hanger, and after school the children listened to shows sponsored by breakfast cereal manufacturers and sent in for secret code rings.

But the changes that came to America during World War II were so profound, numerous, and varied that understanding them is the focus of graduate school programs and academic dissertations. The war was a tragedy of colossal proportions that nonetheless spurred technological innovation and, ultimately, undreamed-of prosperity. But it was also responsible for upwards of fifty million deaths, more than half of them noncombatants. Both sides killed civilians without hesitation. The cruelty and the carnage were without parallel, and the conflict finally ended with the first (and second) deployment of an atomic bomb.

With the onset of the war, business as usual ground to a halt for most of the country's population. The hopes and dreams of individuals and institutions were tabled. As the Depression began to ease and people started to pull themselves up, Lutheran SMOs begun planning for new programs and new facilities. Now those plans had to be shelved. Children in the orphanages planted victory gardens. Staff members of social ministry facilities were drafted, enlisted, or left for higher-paying defense jobs. By 1942 a third of the staff of one Lutheran hospital had entered the military. Unemployment vanished as the country mobilized its industry, producing victory ships, planes, and munitions. Eventually the nation's resources proved to be greater than those of Germany, Japan, and all their allies combined. People swarmed to industrial centers now desperate for their labor, in sharp contrast to the "No Help Wanted" signs of a few years before. As in the First World War, African Americans fled Jim Crow in the South for jobs in the North. Anyone and everyone came to where the jobs were, from West Virginia and the Carolinas to Akron and Chicago and Detroit, with or without skills and training—a human tide permanently altering city landscapes and American demographics.

The old societal barriers broke down. Whites worked side by side in factories with African Americans. Rosie the Riveter proved that women could do "men's work," and her sisters joined the armed forces as Wacs or Waves. Everyone managed to make do with less. Young couples married in haste, then spent long, lonesome months an ocean apart. Posters warned that "loose lips sink ships." Churches were full every Sunday. Parents and spouses were worried about their loved ones serving in the military and prayed for their safety. Members of congregations upheld each other and gave people strength to endure the trying times.

People were hardly enthusiastic about joining the overseas conflict, and Lutheran denominations shared this reluctance to be involved. That began to change when newspapers told of the Nazi persecution of Jews, Catholics, and fellow Lutherans. Then German blitzkrieg attacks conquered neutral countries—Denmark, Norway, Belgium, and Holland. France was defeated and occupied. Finally, on December 7, 1941, Pearl Harbor was attacked, and the United States entered the war. Resolved the Norwegian Lutheran Church of America after the nation entered the conflict: "We recognize that in the present titanic struggle there are principles involved that are essential to human welfare and closely allied with the freedom of conscience and of worship that we value so highly. Therefore, we urge our members to manifest their loyalty by giving full support to the war efforts of their country with their substance and, if necessary, with their lives."[11]

The National Lutheran Council and the Army and Navy Commission of the Lutheran Church–Missouri Synod continued the work they had begun in 1934, but now many more Lutheran pastors were seeking certification from them as they offered their services as military chaplains. The council also assumed responsibility for the so-called orphaned missions that had been started by German and Finnish Lutheran missionaries in Germany's African colonies. Those missions had been cut off from their European founders because of the war.

In 1941, before the United States entered the war, the council surveyed forty-two military camps and forty-eight adjacent communities, and then started the Lutheran Service Commission, establishing centers in a number of cities for servicemen and servicewomen and encouraging local congregations to keep in touch with their members who were serving in the armed forces. Three years later forty-four Lutheran pastors were serving in these centers. A special fund appeal raised a half million dollars to fund the work, as well as to support the orphaned missions and to give aid to refugees from the war.[12]

Though they still could not find agreement on doctrinal issues,[13] American Lutherans were finding ways to work together in meeting human need. Several Lutheran SMOs supported by people from different Lutheran denominations were cobbled together in the 1940s under administrative umbrellas that set standards for the participating agencies and helped them avoid unnecessary competition or duplication of efforts. These inter-Lutheran SMOs also resolved a fairly simple but vexing problem when they realized that it was more effective for a combined body, rather than a dozen different Lutheran churches, to negotiate its work with the non-Lutheran world.

In 1887 church leaders in Denver, Colorado, had begun the Charity Organization Society (which became Community Funds, the forerunner of today's United Way). This organization coordinated services and fund raising for twenty-two agencies. Potential contributors did not find themselves having to contend with a multitude of worthy causes all asking for their money. The funds also provided a degree of community oversight for charitable groups. Lutheran SMOs, by the 1930s, were anxious to participate, but fund leaders were reluctant to include independent yet similar programs that used the word "Lutheran" in their titles. The differences between Lutheran groups might have been important to denominational leaders, but the world couldn't care less! Lutheran SMOs wondered how they could structure themselves so as to qualify for Community Fund membership and largesse.

In late 1936 Lutheran laypeople in Chicago reacted to this problem by forming the Lutheran Church Charities Committee. Membership on the committee included representatives from the American Lutheran Church, the Augustana Synod, the Danish Lutheran Synod, the Lutheran Church–Missouri Synod, the Norwegian Lutheran Church, and the United Lutheran Church in America. Under the label of the Lutheran Church Charities Committee, givers to the Community Fund could provide assistance to ministries serving the needs of children, hospitals, hospices, the aging, and families. In the 1940s and 1950s similar groups, usually statewide in scope, were organized in Minnesota, North Dakota, Washington, New York, Colorado, Oregon, and Nebraska.

Inter-Lutheran efforts for social ministry work and military chaplaincies were characterized as "cooperation in externals" by the Lutheran Church–Missouri Synod leaders as a way of getting around the denomination's conservative theology and refusal even to pray with other Lutherans.[14] John W. Behnken, the synod's president, wrote a policy statement in 1941 declaring that his church could not cooperate "in any form in the dissemination of the gospel." Any cooperation had to be confined to "externals," such as relief to orphaned missionaries and work among soldiers and sailors. Still others contended that the term suggested that social ministry was an external matter to Christian faith and the life of the church. Not so, Missouri Synod welfare leader Henry F. Wind insisted in 1943. Social ministry is a sign of the presence of the grace of God and a necessary fruit that grows out of faith.[15]

Changes to the Orphanage System

By the 1940s ten thousand children were living in seventy-three Lutheran orphanages. But something was affecting those institutions. One Pennsylvania home had 350 children in 1936, but in eight years that number had dropped to 183, and in 1962 the orphanage was closed. The needs were not any less, but they were different. Traditional family life in America had been disrupted by the war, not only because parents had been separated as a result of military service, but also because so many women had entered the workforce. As a result, husbands might be working the night shift in the factories, wives the day shift, putting families at risk and leaving the children to fend for themselves. Social workers and psychologists were seeing increased numbers of people affected by divorce, abuse, and delinquency.

Social ministry leaders were questioning the value of the orphanage system. In 1940 the Lutheran Welfare Conference in America called for the use of institutional care of children only as a last resort. The conference, expressing a preference for foster home placement or returning children to their original homes, encouraged welfare agencies to place a greater emphasis on restoring family life. But a White House conference thirty years before had declared that dependent children normally should be placed in foster homes rather than in orphanages. Many Lutheran orphanages were still functioning in the 1960s! Why?

The solid stability of bricks was one reason. Orphanages had large buildings and long-established organizational structures. It was not easy to find another use for those buildings or convince members of the board of directors that change was necessary. After all, they probably reasoned, orphaned children touched the hearts of faithful church members who supported the institution. People could always see where their money was going when they attended homecoming functions that included tours of the facilities. No such tours were possible with adoptions or foster home placements.

Then there was the matter of the times. Because of a decline in the birthrate during the Depression, and an overall improvement in health in the 1940s, fewer children were true orphans. But the orphanages were not abandoned. Many turned to the care of emotionally disturbed youngsters or met the needs of those with physical or mental disabilities. When some large campuses were sold and turned into state-run facilities, SMOs used the proceeds to fund new areas of service. A number of programs for the aging trace their start to such circumstances.

In the 1940s Henrietta Lund, a field consultant for the National Lutheran Council's Division of Welfare, declared that "there are orphanages in this country so badly run they ought to be abolished."[16] Lund contended that the defining words "orphans" and "orphanages" needed to be eliminated, and campus schools should be closed and the children sent to public schools. She was not alone in her criticism. Bertha Paulssen, a refugee from Nazi Germany with extensive social work experience, evaluated one Pennsylvania Lutheran church orphanage in 1941, spending a month on campus before giving her report. The children, she wrote, lived in a military system in which adults enforced their standards through pressure. Many enforced discipline through beatings, which she termed "a declaration of bankruptcy."

Paulssen noted that "the home was conceived in a time when military order and the idea of the barrack dominated the minds of institutional workers." It functioned in "military order with children marching two by two—marching in groups to every function of daily life—like meals, dressing, work." She called for the end of dormitories, the reform of vocational programs taught by people who did not have "the slightest idea how to teach and train children," and the inauguration of recreational activities connecting children with "the world outside."[17]

That Dim and Distant Past

In the dim and distant past with which we began this chapter, the efforts of Lutheran social ministry organizations largely reflected the life and times of their people. Most were simple folk whose ancestors did not come over on the Mayflower or fight in the Revolutionary War. They arrived from Europe for a variety of reasons, and once here they usually settled into communities where the language and the culture were familiar and where they would raise their families and live the rest of their lives. And so they cared for their neighbors and their relatives and went to church most Sundays and had their pastor over for dinner once in a while, and he baptized their children and grandchildren and married their young people and buried their dead. Most did not need a social ministry organization for themselves or their kin, not so long as they and their children could stay healthy and have someone to take care of them when they were sick.

But not everyone could stay healthy, and not everyone had someone to take care of them when they got sick or old and vulnerable. Neighbors and relatives helped, but here and there, as life grew more difficult and complicated, church folk began wondering about better ways of meeting needs. As they read in their Bibles about the Good Samaritan and the Prodigal Son, they and their pastors determined to do what they could to meet the needs where they lived. So they started an orphanage or a home for the aging—not for everyone, at first, but for their neighbors who, like them, had come from far away and settled where they did because they had come from the same homeland, maybe even the same town. A few decades later, as the melting pot of America's population increased, they or their offspring opened the doors of those facilities to their newer neighbors, folks who might have followed other creeds and might have come from other climes and spoke strange tongues. But ultimately they were the reason why Lutheran social ministry organizations today are major providers of care for lost and hurting people in our country. Were it not for them, we'd still be caring just for our own!

For Further Reading

Hale, J. Russell. *Touching Lives through Service: The History of Tressler Lutheran Services 1868–1994*. Mechanicsburg, Pa.: Tressler Lutheran Services, 1994.

Leuking, F. Dean. *A Century of Caring, 1868–1968*. St. Louis: Board of Social Ministry, Lutheran Church–Missouri Synod, 1968.

Ohl, J. F. *The Inner Mission: A Handbook for Christian Workers*. Philadelphia: General Council Publication House, 1911.

6

Bringing Hope and Life

Lutheran Social Ministry Organizations in America since World War II

Robert Duea

The Lutheran response to human needs in the past sixty years continues to witness dramatically to the gospel of Jesus Christ. The growth of the church's system-wide commitment to social justice expresses the Spirit's work in the world of God the Creator.

This chapter describes a few of the trends in social ministry as illustrated by the ministry of particular organizations.[1] It also chronicles the development of a national Lutheran social ministry system, which grew out of independent local missions that had been reaching out and helping individuals, families, and communities. Included in the stories will be portraits of some of the "giants" who contributed to the panorama. Creating these ministries without blueprints and textbooks, they admittedly were making it up as they went along.

Key Features of Lutheran Social Ministry Agencies

A profile of Lutheran health and human services in the United States after World War II would have to include the following observations:

- Hospitals comprised the largest organized component.

- Orphanages and convalescent homes, started by an individual or a congregation, dotted the landscape.
- Lutheran inner mission societies were common in larger communities having a significant Lutheran population.
- International relief and resettlement were getting underway.

The entire organized Lutheran enterprise of helping people in the middle of the twentieth century did not exceed $16 million, with fewer than eight thousand paid staff and ten thousand volunteers. Over the past sixty years, the growth has been explosive. In 2007 Lutheran Services in America (LSA) reported:

> 300 health and human service organizations provide care in thousands of communities in the United States and the Caribbean. Last year, these organizations served more than 6 million unduplicated clients, meaning that they served one in 50 people in the service territory. Utilizing the skill and dedication of a quarter of a million staff and volunteers, LSA member organizations provide services ranging from health care to disaster response, from services for children and families to care for the elderly, from adoption to advocacy.[2]

The collective budget of LSA members, including health care, exceeds $9 billion per year.

The initial funding of these ministries came from the generosity of individuals and congregations who built or bought sites for orphanages and convalescent homes. In the first days of convalescent homes and orphanages, residents often worked for room and board. By working on farms, they could raise their own food. Local funds also built hospitals. As society became more complex and mobile, these sources were inadequate to the task. The needs always outstripped resources. Ministry required new and creative revenues.

Local communities developed Community Chests to bring citizens together to help others. In communities with a significant Lutheran population, the Lutheran programs became recipients of the community fundraising effort. These Community Chests would become United Way, and local boards would fund Lutheran ministries because of their quality and quantity.

With the passage of Medicaid and human service funding in the 1960s, Lutheran organizations began to use government funding. In many states, they became major providers of human services on behalf of the state or county. Lutheran organizations learned how to collaborate with government without denying their origin and faith mission. Government contracting for services drove these agencies to become multimillion-dollar organizations.

The Hill-Burton Act of 1946 (also known as the Hospital Survey and Construction Act) and other federal programs provided capital for building costs. With the imposition of standards of care and regulations, these funding sources were critical to the growth of nonprofit agencies, which could neither tax nor sell stock to raise capital. Program funding was available through block grants to states. Of all of these sources, nothing surpassed the funding put into the hands of poor and sick persons who could now pay for their service through Medicaid.

States also took more responsibility for health and human services by matching federal dollars as well as providing tax funds for programs. Counties that historically had been responsible for the care of the poor and people with disabilities began closing their county-owned and operated institutions, preferring to utilize private nonprofit agencies.

Insurance programs expanded benefits to include mental health and addiction. Through their family counseling and behavioral health services, Lutheran organizations sought and received insurance reimbursement for their care.

Philanthropic foundations also provided an important source of funding in both health care and social ministry organizations. The foundations included national ones like Annie E. Casey, Atlantic Philanthropies, and Robert Wood Johnson as well as local family foundations often couched within community foundations.

In the last decade of the twentieth century, "customers," such as adoptive parents, were increasingly expected to pay the full cost of the services they used. The cost of an adoption in 1965 was $600. Today that cost has risen to $25,000 for a domestic adoption and up to $40,000 for international.

The story of funding would not be complete without highlighting "remainder foundations." Lutherans sometimes sold the hospitals they had founded to other organizations—usually health care systems. The proceeds from those sales were put into foundations that have become sizable. The transferred funds provide funding for Lutheran health and social ministry organizations that continue the mission of healing. The most famous of these is Wheat Ridge Ministries.

In 1905, members of St. John Lutheran Church in Denver formed the Evangelical Lutheran Sanitorium Association and purchased twenty acres of property in Wheat Ridge, Colorado, where they built a tent colony for people with tuberculosis. In 1921 they dismantled the tent colony (it had served 950 patients in sixteen years) and replaced it with a pavilion. In 1942, the Wheat Ridge Foundation was established to assist Lutherans in their work with other tuberculosis sanatoria throughout the United States. In 1946 the Evangelical Lutheran Sanatorium Association was reorganized under the Wheat Ridge Foundation. The Lutheran Hospital and Medical Center purchased the sanatorium property in 1960, and proceeds from the sale formed an endowment within the Wheat Ridge Foundation. In 1992 Wheat Ridge Foundation changed its name to Wheat Ridge Ministries. This remainder foundation continues to provide funding for new ministries within the Lutheran system.

Another major source of funding is Thrivent Financial for Lutherans, the successor to Aid Association for Lutherans and Lutheran Brotherhood. As a fraternal benefit society, Thrivent contributes to many institutions within the Lutheran church, including Lutheran Services in America and its constituent agencies. Their Giving Plus program of matching individual contributions has been a major success. In 2008, Thrivent and its subsidiaries earmarked a total of $27.3 million for Giving Plus.

Finally, the health and social ministry organizations are following the lead of higher education by developing their own resource development efforts that feed into perpetual endowments. One of the large social ministry organizations developed a financial plan to enhance its ministries: each year the organization transfers 50 percent of its surplus to its own foundation to be available when needed.

Contributions from congregations and individuals continue to provide critical support for Lutheran social ministry organizations. Whether that support encompasses 5 percent or 50 percent of the budget, it is the key that opens the door in the morning. Such support grows out of respect for the fiscal responsibility that Lutheran agencies have demonstrated. In addition to the congregations' financial generosity, the number of volunteers who have brought their love and skills is beyond calculation.

Domestic Adoption and Child Welfare

Many Lutheran agencies trace their origins to the mid-nineteenth century as orphanages established for children who had lost their parents to illness and death. Dramatic changes in children and family needs since World War II challenged Lutheran social ministry to become more extensive, encompassing both domestic and international arenas. By the end of World War II, the transition from the traditional orphanage was well underway as they changed to long-term homes for sibling groups as well as residential treatment programs for youth. The development of adoption as an important part of Minnesota's child welfare system provides a dramatic example of the Lutheran response to children in need of a home.

At Lutheran Social Services (LSS) of Minnesota, adoption came about as the result of many factors beginning in the 1950s. Back then, an unmarried mother still had little support for keeping her child. The rights of the biological father were not recognized, and most states would terminate parental rights based on the birth mother's signature (or that of her parents if she was under age). The termination of an unwanted pregnancy was still illegal and dangerous. "Hospital placements" were common. Government support was nonexistent except for Aid to Dependent Children. Unmarried and pregnant young women often looked for and found acceptance at maternity homes. Under these circumstances, approximately 80 to 85 percent of young women placed their children for adoption.

Professionals like Clayton Hagen, director of adoption at LSS of Minnesota, framed adoption to be so "natural" that couples wishing to adopt underwent little or no scrutiny. Home studies and other means of "testing" the prospective parents' qualifications diminished in importance. The naturalness of this process also led to "closed" adoptions. Agencies gave parents as little information as possible except for significant health issues.

Adoptions were not secret but celebrated by the adoptive parents and the Lutheran congregations of which they were members. Most of the 1,200 Lutheran congregations in Minnesota had at least one adopted child in their midst during this time. Late in the '60s and early '70s, the numbers of adoptions in Minnesota reached 1,100. Then things changed. Within a few years, the percentage of children kept by their mothers reversed. LSS of Minnesota went from placing children in a few months to a waiting list that could take nine years.

What happened? First, the Supreme Court made abortion legal in *Roe v. Wade*. Second, changes in economics and social acceptance enabled more and more women to stay in their parental homes or communities. The critical shift came with society's belief that being a single parent was acceptable, a shift brought on by the increasing number of divorces. Third, courts asserted the parental rights of the biological father, requiring identification and contact. For example, in a small community in western Minnesota, a teenage girl came to LSS seeking help in placing her child. The interview disclosed that she had met the father of her child at the county fair but otherwise had no contact with him. The worker had to identify him and track him down in Las Vegas to get his voluntary termination of parental rights. When he balked, the mother decided to keep the child.

In the mid-1980s, pressure by birth parents to participate in the selection of adoptive parents increased dramatically. It began on the East and West Coasts, as agencies vied for placement of a decreasing number of children. Once the agencies began to accommodate the wishes of birth parents, open adoption became accepted. Now the birth parents actively selected the adoptive parents and often met with them to provide a continuing relationship with their biological child.

The openness of the Lutheran agencies to adapt and cultivate programs for children in spite of dramatically changing conditions enabled necessary ministries to develop. While many adoption agencies closed or refused to open their procedures, Lutheran agencies sought to make it a healthy process for each member of the triad: birth parents, adoptive parents, and child. These agencies saw this development as the reemergence of the extended family raising a child. Today, in most Lutheran agencies, prospective parents must agree to open adoption before they are accepted into the program.

INTERNATIONAL ADOPTION

In the 1940s Americans attempted to rescue children victimized by the war in Europe, but immigration quotas frustrated their efforts. President Truman signed a directive shortly after the war to issue visas to war orphans. In 1946 the first sixty-seven displaced children left Germany. Upon arriving in New York in May 1946, five of the sixty-seven children were assigned to

Lutheran agencies. By 1953, when that program ended, 4,177 children had been admitted and placed. The modern era of international adoption of children had begun.

Following the cessation of hostilities in Korea in 1953, Harry and Bertha Holt loaded airplanes with abandoned and orphaned children. Many of these children were not accepted by the Korean culture because they were Amerasian, the offspring of Korean mothers and American fathers in the U.S. military. "Through their deep Christian faith and fierce determination, they [the Holts] *showed the world that adoption is a banner of love, not a badge of shame*."[3] LSS of Minnesota began an active international adoption program in cooperation with Korea Social Service in the late '60s.

A few Lutheran agencies have developed and invested in programs and staff in Eastern Europe, South and Central America, and Southeast Asia. In October 2000 President Clinton signed the Intercountry Adoption Act, the U.S. implementation of the Hague Convention on International Adoption. Leadership in Lutheran social ministry organizations throughout the United States urged Congress to pass this legislation as well as the Citizenship Act, which allowed children adopted from other countries to become citizens immediately. That same year, Lutheran agencies formed the Lutheran Adoption Network with the purpose of giving additional agencies access to children needing homes as well as expanding countries of origin.

International adoption programs are subject to national interests and are difficult to sustain on a consistent basis. The numbers of children adopted from China and Russia rose from zero in the early 1990s to over five thousand per country annually by 2000. As recently as 2007, the numbers had slowed considerably as a result of political controversies and changed international relations. In spite of the high costs and difficult international issues, the desire for adoptive children continues to increase domestically and internationally.

Opportunities for ministry also developed in the area of foster care. States' policies of removing children from their homes and placing them in foster care for their protection resulted in enormous numbers of children staying in foster care beyond the intended short term. As the phenomenon of foster care "drift" developed, states came under increasing criticism for the questionable safety and high cost of the foster care system. Lawsuits increased, and in some cases the courts began to run the child welfare systems through "consent decrees." Many Lutheran organizations became partners with the state through major contracts to improve the foster care system and to provide for permanent placement of children with special needs. While these were opportunities for ministry, the involvement imperiled organizations financially.

In all of this, Lutheran social ministry organizations always kept their gospel-rooted mission central to their services. Mistakes were made, children were hurt, and families were broken. Yet the number of children living in loving "forever families" was beyond the most profound vision of those who approved the initial movement of sixty-seven children from war-torn Europe in 1946.

SERVICES TO PEOPLE WITH DISABILITIES

In the years following World War II, organizations dedicated to helping persons with disabilities came together with agencies providing child welfare and family services to form multiservice agencies. The stories of Bethesda Lutheran Homes and Services in Watertown, Wisconsin, and Lutheran Social Services of Wisconsin and Upper Michigan provide examples.

Bethesda's origin goes back to *Kinderfreund* (children's friend) societies that developed in Europe in the 1800s. Through immigrants, this ministry found root in Watertown, Wisconsin, where in 1923 it became known as Bethesda. During and after World War II, Bethesda provided a place for people with disabilities to live, even while the agency struggled with its own financial and staff shortages. The center broke through its hard times in the late '30s and began a period of building expansion in the '40s and program expansion in the '60s.

The Reverend Clarence Golisch, who became superintendent in 1950, reported, "The trend in secular circles is away from institutions, even though many states are building larger and improved facilities. I believe in providing for community facilities for retaining these children in normal channels of living as much as possible."[4] Bethesda established its first community-based group home in 1961.

Increased regulation by government led to a near-fatal crisis for organizations like Bethesda. Under the direction of Alexander Napolitano, who brought business and health care administrative skills to the center, Bethesda met the challenge. In addition, the availability of government funding through Medicaid and matching state funds enabled organizations like Bethesda to continue their ministries. Bethesda even expanded its services into multiple states. In order to bring its expertise to local communities and congregations, Bethesda established the National Christian Resource Center in the mid-'80s. For the past twenty years Dr. David Geske has helped Bethesda expand and adapt, absorbing Good Shepherd in California and taking on an international mission to people with disabilities in Eastern Europe. The organization had a budget of over $137 million in 2007.

In the early '80s, Lutheran Social Services of Wisconsin and Upper Michigan met with parents of disabled adults and with state representatives. The result was establishing group homes so that persons with disabilities could live in community rather than in one of the state's three large institutional centers or a local nursing home. The state began to match Medicaid funds for a program called Community Integration Program (CIP). With the approval of the board and central leadership, LSS staff began to buy homes or build them from scratch.

Starting with one group home in Milwaukee, LSS has opened over 150 residential homes ranging from six-bed residences to supported apartments for hundreds of people with disabilities. By 2008 the agency was serving 102 residential programs in 44 communities and 2,800 clients in diverse programs, including residential and drop-in support, birth-to-three services, supported employment, day services, and guardianships. The services include assisting persons who are quadriplegic and ventilator-dependent to live in their own homes. The mission was to create a least-restrictive environment for each person.

In this world of people with disabilities, "miracles" are common. LSS relates each of the programs to a local congregation. LSS clients and staff often occupy the front pew at Sunday morning worship, a witness to all who are present. Dedicated Christian staff and volunteers enable totally dependent persons, many incontinent and unable to feed themselves, to live in a home, cook, maintain personal hygiene, use public transportation, and work in the community.

As the end of the twentieth century approached, another miracle was occurring that would challenge the disability service system to be creative and resilient. As a result of medical advances and improved care and nutrition, people with severe disabilities are, for the first time, looking forward to normal life expectancies. Many parents have taken some comfort in the fact that they would outlive their children with severe disabilities; parents now face the fact that their children may outlive them. Lutheran social ministry organizations are working to help parents address this issue.

Through the work of Bethesda and LSS of Wisconsin, persons with disabilities are no longer hidden away. They are entering public classrooms, occupying offices, and contributing to our society. Both of these organizations have had active advocacy programs, urging national and state legislatures to improve accessibility and opportunities for persons with special needs.

Within Lutheran Services in America, the organizations working with people with disabilities have formed a Disability Network. The network encompasses thirteen national and state agencies providing support to more than twelve thousand persons in thirty states and the Virgin Islands. The network, recognizing its historic voice in advocating for people with disabilities, placed a full-time person in the Office for Public Policy in Washington, D.C., in 2004.

Immigration and Refugee Services

Following World War I, the golden years that had welcomed "your tired, your poor, your huddled masses yearning to be free" were all but ended. Then Hitler and the National Socialist Party rose to power in 1933. By 1938, here in the United States, the National Lutheran Council had formed the Lutheran Refugee Services (LRS), and interest in helping the refugees and displaced persons in northern Europe was intense among American Lutherans.

In Europe following World War II, the number of displaced persons led to a massive relief and resettlement effort by the victorious allies. When the constituting convention of the Lutheran World Federation took place in Sweden on June 30, 1947, the representatives learned that one out of every ten Lutherans worldwide was a refugee; in Europe, one of every three displaced persons was a Lutheran. It is no wonder that the first resolution was a call to action. "Like Israel confronting the ruined walls of Jerusalem, we must arise and build . . . immigration and resettlement plans . . . safeguarding the religious life of those displaced persons who belong to the household of our faith."[5] Lutheran resettlement and immigration became the main contractor with the United Nations High Commissioner for Refugees. As a result, immigration and refugee efforts began in the worldwide Lutheran community.

Giants in the resettlement effort during and following World War II were Clarence Krumholz, Paul Empie, and Cordelia Cox. Krumholz, general secretary of the Board of Social Missions of the United Lutheran Church in America, deserves to be known as the father of Lutheran refugee services and a pioneer in developing the field of Lutheran social ministry. Empie, executive director of the National Lutheran Council, demonstrated courageous and visionary leadership that enabled so much of the United States to respond to resettlement efforts. Cox, the first director of Lutheran Refugee Services, coordinated a system of committees throughout the country that developed assurances for jobs and housing. The first displaced persons arrived in New York on October 30, 1948, the forerunners of thirty-five thousand persons resettled in the next three years.

In 1956 students and factory workers rose up against the Soviet regime in Hungary. Radios picked up the last broadcast from Budapest. "Civilized people of the world, in the name of liberty and solidarity, we are asking you to help. Our ship is sinking. The light vanishes. . . . Listen to our cry. . . . People of the world save us. S-O-S! Help! Help! God be with you and with us!"[6] Again, the Lutheran community responded—this time resettling 21,500 Hungarians through Lutheran congregations.

Starting in the early '60s, the Lutheran community saw numerous opportunities to test its commitment to resettling people who were not Lutheran. Many refugees flowed into Hong Kong, and thousands of people fled Cuba for Florida. The expulsion of 75,000 Indians from Uganda by Idi Amin in 1972 brought a new sense of urgency. Many of these refugees were either Muslim or Hindu. The National Lutheran Council, Lutheran families, congregations, and local LSS agencies responded. People arriving from foreign communities found a warm welcome by individuals and congregations that openly witnessed to their faith but made no demand that their faith become the faith of the immigrant.

The Lutheran response evolved into what became known as Lutheran Immigration and Refugee Service (LIRS). Events in Southeast Asia in the mid-1970s led LIRS to change. In 1975 the U.S. government mobilized military bases as temporary "camps" for hundreds of thousands of fleeing refugees and called voluntary agencies into partnership. The direct funding of voluntary agencies by the State Department made it possible for LIRS to place in LSS agencies regional consultants who could coordinate the work of resettling refugees from the military camps as well as Guam and the Philippines. As large numbers of unaccompanied minors moved into the camps, LIRS formed an emergency foster care program with twenty-four LSS agencies.

LIRS has faced a number of key decision-making points that have profoundly affected the development of the organization and its place in society:

- In the mid-50s, the National Lutheran Council realized its work for displaced Lutherans was essentially completed. Did that mean that LIRS would go out of business? Paul Empie envisioned a broader mission for the agency.
- With the fall of Saigon in April 1975, the Ford Administration decided (despite public opposition) to take in those Vietnamese who had supported the United States. The number would eventually grow to one million. LIRS decided to become a partner with the government, and that decision marked the first time LIRS received public funding.
- Late in 1975, LIRS made another decision to collaborate with existing social ministry organizations rather than develop its own national delivery system.
- In 1980–81, Central America erupted, and for the first time the United States faced the challenge of uninvited refugees. These became known as the Asylum Seekers. LIRS decided to use church funding to establish a program for asylum work. That program is the only one among the voluntary agencies that continue its work in 2008.

During the first decade of the twenty-first century, undocumented immigrants are the subject of national debate. The last major attempt at dealing with persons in the United States without proper authorization was in 1986, when Congress passed an amnesty law to deal with an estimated three million persons in the United States. Twenty-two years later, the number was nearly twelve million. Approximately 40 percent are people who entered the country legally and have stayed after their authorization expired. The other 60 percent have entered this country illegally. A large proportion of these undocumented immigrants (estimated to be nearly 50 percent) lives with families who are here legally as citizens or with proper documentation.

LIRS has advocated for a generous welcome for immigrants and refugees with an emphasis on the family. That basic principle has led to consistent support for comprehensive immigration reform. LIRS has affirmed four principles regarding the issue of undocumented immigrants in the United States. LIRS upholds that comprehensive reform must (1) unite families, (2) protect human rights and worker rights, (3) end marginalization and bring people out of the shadows, and (4) provide a path to permanence for undocumented immigrants in the United States.[7]

LIRS lives out its mission in partnership with social ministry organizations across the country. "In response to God's love in Christ, we welcome the stranger, bringing new hope and new life through ministries of service and justice."[8]

Health Care Services

Wherever Lutheran immigrants have gathered in the United States, they have acted out of concern for the health of their community, developing Lutheran hospitals and health care organizations, especially in the North Atlantic states and the Midwest. When health care became more complex and expensive, many of the Lutheran hospitals were sold. Some Lutheran hospitals have continued and are now part of larger health care systems. Nationally, the two dominant Lutheran entities are Fairview Health Services in Minnesota's Twin Cities and Advocate Health Care in the Chicago metropolitan area. This section will trace the development of Advocate Health Care.

In 1995 two faith-based organizations came together to form Advocate Health Care. The first of these, Lutheran General Health Systems, started in 1897, when the Norwegian Lutheran Deaconess Society of Chicago opened a hospital to care for immigrants living in Humboldt Park. In the 1950s, the Evangelical Lutheran Church purchased land to build a new hospital, Lutheran General Hospital, which opened in Park Ridge in 1959. In 1989, Lutheran General merged with Augustana Hospital, which was founded by Swedes in 1884 in Chicago's Lincoln Park.

The second faith-based partner in Advocate is Evangelical Health System, which evolved from hospitals founded by Germans living on Chicago's South Side. This system became affiliated with the United Church of Christ.

One of the noteworthy contributions from Lutheran General was Dr. Frederic Norstad's development of the Institute for Human Ecology. Norstad wrote, "Human Ecology describes man in terms of the essential and dynamic unity of all aspects of his being . . . intellectual, emotional, physical, social and spiritual. It says that ideally, therapy should include a treatment of the total man . . . and he should be treated as part of his environment, with particular attention to his family situation, life calling, employment and to his religious faith." And further, "It is a life view and a way of life directed at healing man's essential illness, which we define as his brokenness."[9] Nowhere was this principle more evident than in the healing team, which included the doctor, the chaplain, and the patient.

Today Advocate Health Care is the largest nonprofit health care delivery system in metropolitan Chicago, encompassing eight hospitals, 3,500 beds, and more than two hundred sites of care. With 24,500 employees and 4,600 affiliated physicians, it has an enormous impact upon the health of thousands of people.[10]

SERVICES TO THE ELDERLY

At a 1992 meeting of a House of Representatives committee that was dealing with an important piece of legislation concerning the elderly, a committee staff person said, "If you want to talk to experts in providing care for our senior citizens, make sure you get testimony from the Lutherans—they are the best at it."[11]

This section will describe three models of services to the elderly. The following trends and developments had differing impacts on each of these models.

- Increase in life expectancy and the relative independence of the elderly into their nineties
- Nursing home regulation (government involvement in quality of care)

- Multiple levels of service, from independent living to skilled nursing care
- Government and social ministry organization (SMO) partnerships (where SMOs are providers of service, and the government is the payer)
- Church relationships (recognition and affiliation of SMOs as integral to the life and work of the church)
- Campus-bound and community-based services

The Evangelical Lutheran Good Samaritan Society is today the largest Lutheran SMO serving the elderly, but originally it had a different purpose. In the early 1920s, the Good Samaritan Society of North Dakota conducted a fund-raising effort to assist a young boy with polio. The effort was so successful that the Society was able to invest the $2,000 surplus into its mission of helping individuals with disabilities. In 1923, the Society opened its first home in Arthur, North Dakota.

By the 1930s, after opening thirty care centers, the Society's financial difficulties forced it to reorganize. In 1937, Lutheran Homes and Hospital Society acquired most of Good Samaritan's service locations. By 1940, what remained of the Society was four homes and most of the debt. As World War II began, the Good Samaritan Society decided to rebuild and dedicate its service to the elderly. Within twelve years of the reorganization, the Good Samaritan Society had grown to thirty-two homes in seven states and had managed to resolve its debt problem. Most of the new homes were converted mansions and hospitals.

The early 1950s marked the beginning of government involvement through funding and new regulations. The Hill-Burton Act now made construction funding available. While the Good Samaritan Society leadership initially resisted outside funding, it eventually used these funds, especially as licensing and regulations forced changes in how care was provided.

In January 1965, the historic amendments to the Social Security Act created Medicare and Medicaid. The world of the Good Samaritan Society and other Lutheran SMOs changed. Over the next forty years and beyond, the sources of income for most nursing homes shifted from 100 percent private-pay (charging the people who use the services) and contributions to 90 percent Medicare. In 1968, the federal government enacted the Federal Fair Housing Act and with it Housing and Urban Development programs.

While Good Samaritan maintains its independent culture, the agency has developed two partnerships that have transformed it. First, partnership with the government enabled the agency to use government funds. While this partnership did not alter Good Samaritan's religious mission and vision, it did change the management of the agency's homes through regulation and licensing. Second, the agency collaborated with Lutheran churchwide bodies. In 1986, the Good Samaritan Society became accredited by what is now the Evangelical Lutheran Church in America (ELCA). Later it became a full partner in Lutheran Services in America.

Like many Lutheran SMOs, Good Samaritan primarily traces its roots to one person. August "Dad" Hoeger helped organize Good Samaritan and then kept the agency functioning through a depression, a world war, and the ins and outs of government regulation and funding. In histories, he is variously acclaimed or criticized.-

On yet another front a very different model for establishing services to the elderly was developing. That model was personified by John M. Mason. He had been called to the staff of the Evangelical Lutheran Church (ELC) Department of Charities located in Minneapolis, later becoming the executive of its successor in the American Lutheran Church (ALC). While August Hoeger had been prolific in establishing residences for elderly on behalf of a society of individual Lutherans, John Mason was equally prolific in establishing residences on behalf of a national church and local congregations. In the ELC and ALC Mason was the Johnny Appleseed of nursing homes. He helped establish approximately 125 homes from New York to Hawaii. Most of these were owned and operated by clusters of congregations.

In time, the Mason model underwent major changes. Eventually the ALC divested itself of much of its responsibility regarding nursing homes. In some cases, the nursing homes continued to be owned by an association of congregations, and many continue to thrive today. In other cases, homes owned by the national church were turned over to a group of local congregations.

There is yet a third model of services to the elderly. In the last thirty years of the twentieth century, member agencies of LSS began to develop services to the ever-growing population of elderly persons. Tressler Lutheran Service Associates provides an excellent and successful example. Under the leadership of David Bollinger and James Raun at Tressler Lutheran Services,

LSS of the Central Pennsylvania Synod developed services to the elderly in central Pennsylvania and Maryland. They used funds from the sale of the Tressler Lutheran Home for Children as a pledge to obtain federal funds for building seven nursing homes in the early '70s. This expansion into residential care for the elderly as well as community-based programs continued through the subsequent administrations of Harold Haas, Thomas Hurlocker, and Daun McKee. Today, Diakon Lutheran Social Ministries is the successor to Tressler Lutheran Services and Lutheran Services Northeast (an earlier merger of Lutheran Welfare Services of Northeast Pennsylvania and Lutheran Home at Topton). Diakon remains a major provider of services to the elderly in Pennsylvania and Maryland.

Phenomenal growth in services for the elderly has occurred in many different Lutheran SMOs across the country. Perhaps the dominant issue in the past two decades has been the location of these ministries. On the one hand, the community-based LSS agencies have been developing services to the elderly in the community. On the other hand, the traditional campus-bound nursing homes have expanded beyond residential services to a continuum of care as well as moved off-campus into communities. The two have met there, sometimes combining forces and other times competing with some friction, but still, as a collective ministry, providing the highest quality services to the elderly.

Housing, Disaster Relief, and Other Services

Housing is one of several other services that Lutheran organizations have been helping to provide. Included in this category is housing for seniors and persons with disabilities, and affordable units. The *2007 AAHSA Ziegler 100 Report* indicates that seven of the fifty largest housing providers are Lutheran.[12] If just the housing portions of Lutheran social ministries were combined, the sum would make the Lutheran system the largest nonprofit provider of housing in the United States.

The largest agency in the Lutheran system is the Evangelical Lutheran Good Samaritan Society, with over twenty thousand units. The next largest are Diakon Lutheran Social Ministries in Pennsylvania, Front Porch in California, Lutheran Senior Services in Missouri, Ecumen and Augustana Care in Minnesota, and Lutheran Life Communities in Illinois.

Front Porch (a self-described "community of communities") is an example of the development of social ministry in areas of the country where a Lutheran presence is marginal. The agency came into being in 1999, when California Lutheran Home and Community Services joined forces with other like-minded organizations. In southern California, Front Porch manages eleven full-service retirement communities serving three thousand people; in Louisiana and Florida, Front Porch operates two adult living communities serving three hundred seniors.

Urban development, as seen through the ministry of Bethel New Life in Chicago, has also been a focus of Lutheran social ministries. After the riots of the late '60s and early '70s, members of Bethel Lutheran Church were committed to rebuilding West Garfield Park on Chicago's West Side. In 1979, the congregation purchased and restored a three-flat apartment building. Under the leadership of Mary Nelson, Bethel New Life has grown to include a thousand new units of affordable housing. As a multiservice program, it has assisted in placing over seven thousand people in living-wage jobs. The organization itself employs over 450 staff.

Family Counseling/Behavioral Health has been a core service for most Lutheran social ministry organizations over the past fifty years. In response to the intensifying crises in families, Lutheran service organizations opened counseling offices in their agencies as well as in congregations throughout their service areas, and staffed the offices with accredited social workers. Many of these same agencies have added addiction counseling resources to help families cope with alcohol, drug, or gambling addiction. In addition, courts often have turned to Lutheran organizations to help families cope with violence and abuse.

Chaplains from the Lutheran church serve in prisons, in hospitals, and on college campuses. Whenever people are bound to their location or situation, they still need the church and spiritual service. Most major hospitals provide settings for chaplain training programs. Lutheran General Hospital in Park Ridge, Illinois, has distinguished itself as a center for chaplain residency.

Disaster response is coordinated by Lutheran Disaster Response (LDR), a collaborative ministry of the ELCA and the Lutheran Church–Missouri Synod (LCMS). LDR ministers to people who have experienced major disasters (natural and human caused) and endeavors to care for unmet needs. LDR carries out its ministry through local affiliates, Lutheran SMOs that are specially trained and equipped. LSS of the South, one such local affiliate, continues to provide services in Texas, Louisiana, Mississippi, and Alabama after hurricanes Katrina and Rita.

Advocacy for justice has been a part of the Lutheran social ministry system for years. The ELCA and its predecessors have supported a number of state offices of advocacy, some of which are within LSS agencies. Some social ministry organizations employ government relations staff. On the national level, the Lutheran Office for Public Policy in Washington, D.C., has been the national voice for Lutheran Service in America.

The diverse range of services provided by Lutheran SMOs simply reinforces the great magnitude and quality of Lutheran social ministry in the post–World War II era. The creativity they embody is a testimony to the many people of faith who believe the church lives in the world rather than outside of it.

Cooperation within Social Ministry

In 1918 the various Lutheran churches in the United States came together to form the National Lutheran Council to coordinate Lutheran work. The council continued until the church mergers of the early '60s, which led in 1967 to the formation of the Lutheran Council in the United States (LCUSA).

LCUSA took on the cooperative work in immigration and refugee services as well as social ministry, which itself took advantage of the talents of a nine-person group called the LS/3 Policy Committee. This committee operated in that time of landmark government legislation in the delivery and funding of health and human services. Part of the committee's work was to find ways for the three largest Lutheran churches to cooperate, a task complicated by sometimes conflicting theologies. The committee also developed criteria for affiliation of SMOs. LCUSA served in this role until 1988, when the ELCA was formed, merging the ALC, LCA, and American Evangelical Lutheran Church. The leadership in each of the formerly separate denominations' national offices assumed the cooperative work between the new ELCA and the LCMS.

In order to foster a spirit of cooperation among the social ministry organizations, several associations sprang up, each with its own gathering point, to discuss common concerns and provide opportunity for reflection and renewal. Executives of the agencies came together in 1975 as a Coalition of Executives. Luthard Gjerde, president of LSS of Minnesota, provided early leadership; subsequent leaders include Robert Duea, Richard Eissfeldt, and James Raun. In 1976, the Lutheran Association of Housing Ministries and the Association of Administrators of Lutheran Services with the Aging organized. In 1990, the two merged to become the National Association of Lutheran Ministries with the Aging (NALMA), for which Richard Goebel provided staff leadership. While these steps brought the SMO groups closer together, they continued to be quite independent and in some cases competitors.

To the outside world, and even within the Lutheran church, the ministry of the SMOs went unnoticed because there was no system. In the meantime, public sectors were recognizing national associations—such as Catholic Charities USA, Child Welfare League of America, Alliance for Children and Families, and United Way of America—as experts and inviting them into arenas of public policy formation.

Through a series of steps, Lutheran Services in America was born on April 18, 1997. Nelson Meyer was elected as the first chair and Joanne Negstad its initial president and CEO. In its vision statement, LSA seeks to "increase the service and witness of God's people in both church and society." Its mission is "to support the members' ministries of service and justice by creating a unified system to build and maintain relationships and resources."[13] The first budget was nearly $1 million, which included loaned staff from the ELCA Church in Society and the LCMS Board for Human Care Ministries.

Lutheran social ministry had now grown into a national system. Once LSA began to document its services and size, it took a seat at the table of Leadership 18 (the eighteen largest human service systems in the country) and emerged at the head of the table according to aggregate budget size. LSA became the largest nonprofit human service delivery system in the country. Within a year, LSA placed its first full-time director of public policy in Washington, D.C. At the same time, it committed itself to retaining a faith focus by inviting Lutheran scholar Foster McCurley to serve as the board's first theologian in residence.

After helping LSA get its start, Negstad resigned in 2001. The board elected Jill Schumann as president and CEO. In a 2007 presentation, Schumann reported that there are approximately "100 pan-Lutheran, 170

ELCA and 30 LCMS organizations providing services in fifty states and the Caribbean. . . . The areas of service include addiction, administration, advocacy, aging, children/youth/family, congregational and chaplaincy, consulting and education, disability, emergency/disaster, grant making, health care, housing and community development, mental health, outreach and support. Under these broad service designations lie 157 sub-categories."[14]

Leadership

In chronicling the development of the Lutheran social ministry system since World War II, it is important to ask: Who were the leaders? What made them stand out and lead? How did they learn to be leaders?

Three arbitrary labels are used here to define leaders by their time or environment as much as by internal qualities. In the early development of social ministry, leaders can be seen as "starters." They began simple organizations limited to a single service or building. Then came the "transitioners," those who followed World War II and served through the mid-'60s. Finally, there were the "complexiters."

The starters might best be exemplified by August Hoeger, the man who established a home for children with disabilities in Arthur, North Dakota. Other leaders repeated this story in community after community. The outstanding leadership quality for them was an absolute faith in the gospel and its imperative to care. A second quality of these leaders was the willingness to take chances. They believed unswervingly that God would provide if they persevered. Seldom, if ever, did they have cash at the ready. Theirs was a simpler world, in which meeting the basic needs of food, clothing, and shelter were central to their mission. They were risk takers. Most of these leaders served their church and neighbor in the last half of the nineteenth century and first half of the twentieth.

The transitioners, those in leadership following World War II, took risks and chances when faced with a new uncertain world marked by incredible numbers of displaced persons. Some of the most courageous leaders emerged from within the National Lutheran Council as it worked to rebuild a shattered Europe. These leaders include Clarence Krumholz, Paul Empie, Cordelia Cox, Henry Whiting, Kenneth Senft, Sister Betty Amstutz, and Leslie Weber.

Starting in the 1950s, a group of transitioners settled into leadership of individual organizations. These individuals include Luthard Gjerde, Benjamin Gjenvick, Frederic "Fritz" Norstad, Lee Wesley, and James Raun. They worked to shift their organizational cultures in order to collaborate with government. They had the responsibility of defining and defending social ministry within the new postwar society. Many took their organizations from single sites and services to multiple sites and services. Words that describe these leaders are "flexible" and "students." They were not trained or educated for what they were about to encounter. They had to learn on the job, and they had to be flexible, adapting or restructuring their organization to meet the challenges of society. Their successes as well as their failures demonstrate their willingness to take risks.

Finally, the complexiters emerged. These leaders take on multiple roles. They know how to identify new leaders within organizations, how to train them, and how to delegate. They know how to develop new services and how to take risks. Most of their organizations have become very large and face the challenges of large companies. Some organizations are becoming global. Leaders in the Lutheran hospital and health care systems include James Skagsbergh at Advocate (Chicago) and Mark Eustis at Fairview (Twin Cities). Other leaders include Carl Thomas (LSS of Michigan), Donald Hallberg and Fred Aigner (LSS of Illinois), Mark Peterson (LSS of Minnesota), Suzanne Wise (Lutheran Family Services of the Carolinas), Kurt Senske (LSS of the South), Daun McKee (Diakon), Ralston Deffenbaugh (LIRS), Jill Schumann (LSA), David Jacox (Mosaic), David Geske (Bethesda Lutheran Home), Kenneth Wheeler (California Lutheran Homes, a Front Porch partner), and Charles Miller (ELCA). The list goes on.

A health and social service system does not become the largest provider in the United States without great leadership. As the Lutheran churches in America looks to train the next generations of pastors, teachers, and social workers, it is fitting to include stories of these leaders—starters, transitioners, and complexiters—and, where possible, even the leaders themselves, in training programs. These leaders were rooted in their faith but held their organizations accountable and visible to the church. They learned how to do their jobs because they never felt they had arrived—they always saw themselves as students. They looked for ways to serve society but also to nurture their staffs. They took risks, and they each took on the role of teacher for one another and for new generations of leaders.

Social Ministry Today and in the Future

The leaders of the organizations highlighted in this chapter have a great deal to say about the future of the Lutheran social ministry endeavor within the United States and globally. Henry Whiting was a leader in the Lutheran Welfare Society of Minnesota during the '40s; sixty years later, his son-in-law Mark Peterson serves as the leader of the same organization (now LSS of Minnesota). In 2005 Peterson observed, "Our mission, centered in the love of Christ, is embraced by our workforce, even though our employees look like Minnesota—Muslim, Lutheran, Jewish, Catholic, no religion, evangelical. Even with this diversity in our workforce and among our volunteers, there is a shared conviction about our work. We are focused on changing lives—supporting those 100,000 persons we serve each year in their journey."[15]

We can no longer live a simple life of service in rural America, for we are a part of a world that is interacting and increasingly interdependent. As our lives unfold, we continue to find human misery and threats to the children of God in such forms as neglect, terrorism, and environmental dangers. The mission and task of Lutheran social ministry will not end until we are lifted up into the arms of God.

For Further Reading

Hoeger, Agnes, and Irma Person. *Ever Forward: The Story of Dad Hoeger.* Sioux Falls, S.D.: Evangelical Lutheran Society, 1996 [1981].

Mason, John M. *The Fourth Generation.* Minneapolis: Augsburg Publishing House, 1978.

Moberg, Marlys Taege. *Treasured Lives: The Story of Bethesda Lutheran Homes and Services.* Watertown, Wis.: Bethesda Lutheran Homes and Services, 2004.

———. *Why Are They So Happy?* Watertown, Wis.: Bethesda Lutheran Homes and Services, 1998.

Norstad, Fredric M. *Presentations: Governance and Philosophy.* Park Ridge, Ill.: Lutheran General Health System, 1971.

Solberg, Richard W. *Open Doors: The Story of Lutherans Resettling Refugees.* St. Louis: Concordia Publishing House, 1992.

Uehling, Carl T. *Hope and Healing.* St. Paul: Lutheran Services in America, 1999.

7

Where Do We Go from Here?

The Changing Context and Commitments in Social Ministry

The Future's Group

Editor's Note

This chapter is the summary of my roundtable discussion with the Future's Group at their February 2008 meeting. The Future's Group is an informal gathering of chief executive officers of Lutheran social ministry organizations (SMOs), including Lutheran Services in America (LSA) and the ELCA's Division for Church in Society. Originally organized in 1980, its purpose has been to serve as a resource for its members and to offer strategies that strengthen the expression of Lutheran social ministry. The discussion included the following executives:

Frederick Aigner, President/CEO, Lutheran Social Services of Illinois
Dave Larson, President/CEO, Lutheran Social Services of Wisconsin and the Upper Peninsula
Rebecca Larson, Executive Director, Church in Society Unit, Evangelical Lutheran Church in America
Daun McKee, President/CEO, Diakon Lutheran Social Ministries
Roberta Nestaas, President/CEO, Lutheran Community Services Northwest
Mark Peterson, President/CEO, Lutheran Social Services of Minnesota

Jill A. Schumann, President/CEO, Lutheran Services in America
Sam Sipes, President/CEO, Lutheran Services of Florida
Mark Stutrud, President, Lutheran Social Services of Michigan

THE IMPORTANCE OF LUTHERAN IDENTITY

Who are we? Though such a seemingly basic question, it invites not just individuals but organizations as well to explore their identity. The Future's Group focused its attention on the question of identity more than on any other. They began their discussion with a metaphor about oaks and bamboos. Oak communities are those with memory, tradition, and deep roots. Our Lutheran tradition places us among the oaks. Some of the newer churches and organizations are like bamboos; they have shallow roots but grow quickly and spread out. Will the oaks die out and the bamboos take over, or will the bamboos expire because their spiritual roots do not penetrate deeply? How do issues like these affect the way Lutheran social ministry organizations face the future?

Luther distinguished the church from all other gatherings as the "assembly of people among whom the gospel is purely preached and the holy sacraments are administered according to the gospel" (Article VII of the Augsburg Confession). The Word and sacraments are the "deep roots" of the church that set us free to serve the neighbor. Dave Larson voiced his thoughts this way: "God's action to us through the sacraments drives, undergirds, defines, and uplifts all social ministry expressions of the church." Member Fred Aigner shared his thoughts about the gospel and service: "I have come to believe that the social ministry expressions of the church are the fullest and loveliest manifestations of a response to the gospel. While the works of SMOs do not contribute to our salvation, they are a reliable mark of a Christian's experience of a God of grace. In fact, I can think of no better response to the gospel, no more trustworthy sense of the encompassing sweep of God's will for us."

As we have seen in earlier chapters of this book, responding to the gospel through a life of service to the neighbor is key to the work of the Lutheran SMOs. That neighbor can literally be the person next door or a person or entire community many "doors" away. Moreover, as we have seen, caring on a larger scale requires larger caring communities, communities that may be structured as congregations, synods of the church, social ministry organizations, and churchwide agencies. These caring communities serve the needs of others through a host of direct services and through advocacy on behalf of the vulnerable before various levels of governments.

God calls us to serve the neighbor. In Jill Schumann's words, God's call "requires interweaving the three strands of Micah 6:8. Yes, we need to love kindness—to tend to one another's immediate needs, to provide services. But we also need to do justice—to commit to changing our attitudes and structures that perpetuate deep problems. We need to provide these services and do that justice in a humble walk with our God, focused on the radical nature of the gospel and on the complexity and simplicity of the call to love and serve our neighbor."

Guiding our church's incarnational involvement in the world is Luther's theology of the cross. That God reveals divine action, identity, and will in the suffering of Christ inevitably leads us to people in need. Pursuing that direction calls us individually and collectively to put our energy, our finances, our talents, and our lives on the line. It requires of us the highest quality of service because we do it to the glory of the God who became one of us and gives all our lives grace.

Making that grace visible is a challenge. Dave Larson believes strongly that "God's grace is often most visibly evident to the public in social ministry." As the SMOs serve a variety of needs, as they partner with government and other organizations to serve the common good, and as they advocate publicly on behalf of the vulnerable, these organizations provide a tangible expression of the church's incarnational involvement in the public arena.

But what of the staff who provide the care? Social ministry organizations need staff who are talented in their positions but also who meet qualifications set by federal and state governments. They seek employees who are licensed or certified for their positions, who are diligent in record keeping, finance, accounting, and management. The best-qualified person available may or may not be Lutheran or Christian. Confessional tests are neither possible nor desirable. Nevertheless, boards and managers of SMOs consider the work of the whole organization to be a vocation, a calling based on the gospel of Jesus Christ. The religious affiliation of individual staff members does not diminish that sense of vocation or the faith-based mission statements that define and guide the organization.

Through the language of spirituality, many staff—Lutheran, non-Lutheran, and non-Christian—often find deep and profound meaning in their work. Involvement of staff in the spiritual dimensions of their own personhood and of those they serve contributes to the mission of the SMO and enhances the welfare of the community. Roberta Nestaas reflected on the discussions that have taken place in her agency, discussions that have been characterized as "invigorating and renewing." She tells of her experience like this: "Recently, our theologian in residence reflected with our leadership team on our vocational call in the context of three major religious traditions: Jewish, Muslim, and Christian. Our staff is diverse in ethnic and religious affiliation and appreciated his respect for their diversity."

The employment of staff for their talents and certification rather than their confession is appropriate. Social ministry is about ministering to people in society, not exclusively people in the church, and it is a ministry not unique to the Lutheran tradition. Faith-based charities of the Jewish and Roman Catholic traditions, for example, also serve persons not of their faith. Working in partnerships with many of these ministries of other traditions strengthens the service to society as well as honors God, the Creator of us all.

No matter how many others perform similar ministries, our goal is always to be authentic to the gospel of Jesus Christ and to our Lutheran identity. Wrestling with the meaning of that identity leads to personal and organizational growth, as Nestaas has observed over the span of her career.

> In 1980 a pastor asked me, "What is Lutheran about Lutheran Social Services?" I do not recall my response but in reality, I had not a clue. . . . This question set me on my own path to discover the connection. It was the beginning of my involvement in Bible studies with clergy. Those studies led to preaching in Lutheran churches throughout the region, as well as informally pursuing theological education through publications and workshops. Personally, this led to theological thinking beyond social ministry, and I am grateful for this path of spiritual knowledge and growth. I have also learned not to give pat answers about our Lutheran identity. If pressed, I would probably quote Matthew 25 and talk about how we encounter the face of Christ in all those we serve. However, the conversation is more valuable than a simplistic answer.

Conversation about the church and social ministry, especially as we experience the relationships differently in various geographic areas in North America, is related to the history between church and service agencies around the globe. Rebecca Larson describes her observation:

> I have been involved in an international project on *diaconia* that is bringing together experiences from different parts of the world. In Europe, including in the historic Lutheran countries, there are very low levels of church membership and/or engagement in social ministry. In these situations, diaconal institutions have grown up on principles very unconnected with the church in many cases. People value and support these institutions and see in them the presence of the church. In Africa and Asia (and differently in Latin America) there is total integration of diaconal and church work. It is understood as one and the same. Sorting out these relationships between the church and SMOs in North America is critical for the future.

Maintaining Lutheran Identity

SMOs face many challenges in their commitment to maintain their Lutheran identity while simultaneously presenting the church's face to the public. One of those realities is the public face itself. The ministry sometimes requires providing care to people with whom some congregational members have difficulty identifying. Other times, a Lutheran agency might reach its capacity in a nursing home when a member of a nearby congregation requires residential service. Inability to provide care for Lutherans can strain relationships.

Other challenges develop from demographics among Lutherans. In some areas where Lutheran immigrants settled years ago, a healthy percentage of Lutheran congregations do recognize that the organizations are their church serving the neighbor. In other areas, particularly in those where Lutherans do not make up a large segment of the population and where the congregations themselves struggle to survive, Lutheran social ministry organizations feel remote, even unrecognized, and separated from congregational interests. Ironically, some people outside the church know nothing about the Lutheran congregations but speak of the local social ministry organization simply as "Lutheran."

Another reality that challenges Lutheran identity is demographic change in society itself. While the SMOs serve people from diverse racial and cultural backgrounds, many Lutheran congregations are dying because their own diversity is not proportional to the communities around them. The fewer congregations in the area, the less "Lutheran" means to the public. Losing that identity can erode the SMO's foundation and mission and its ability to serve. Diversity is not a social ministry issue per se but one for the church's congregations to address in their mission and ministry. The interaction between congregations and SMOs is integral to ministry. Visibility of this interaction witnesses to the gospel of Jesus Christ in both stable and changing neighborhoods. Together congregations and SMOs provide an identity to the public.

Whether or not there exists a density of Lutherans in a geographical area, however, many SMO leaders feel some language changes would assist their acceptance into the church family. Conversations between congregations and SMOs imply they are two separate realities: congregations are the church, and SMOs are simply an "arm of the church." In addition to the SMOs feeling left out, the language does not help members of the public understand that the SMOs are the church serving the neighbor. Moreover, inconsistencies seem to exist among congregations (and some synods of the ELCA) on whether social ministry is a ministry. The oft-voiced terminology of Word and Sacrament as the only "legitimate" ministry of the church sends a message that our work is peripheral to the church. Would Word and Service send a clearer message about recognizing our work as the church's ministry to the world?

Apart from language, increased mutual hospitality between congregations and SMOs would be beneficial to the whole church. On the one hand, congregations might be more attentive to the SMOs in their areas. Newsletters, sermons, and classes for confirmation and for new members could help members see the ministry of the SMOs as the work of the church and as an opportunity for them to participate in this ministry. On the other hand, SMOs might increase their face-to-face communications with pastors and congregations. Pastors and congregations might gain a better understanding of the complexities of operating large-scale ministries to the public and the demands of government regulations. In reflecting on her work in social ministry, Roberta Nestaas notes, "Over the years I have found myself educating congregations and clergy about our call to do social ministry and its essential role in fulfilling the church's call to do justice and care for our neighbors." SMO leaders might also gain some understanding of the complexities of congregational life, especially when congregations are struggling to survive while SMOs grow larger. Perhaps such mutual hospitality would provide strength for congregations as well as for SMOs.

One area where congregations and SMOs could focus is ministry by youth. Youth are showing in the election campaigns of 2008 that social issues motivate and invigorate them. The ELCA recognizes that its youth mobilize at the point where issues of justice, poverty, and advocacy intersect, where worldly involvement becomes part of the church's unequivocal agenda, where environment and issues of serving the neighbor surface. We need to take this seriously and recognize the resource and capacity of SMOs to engage this important constituency. Capitalizing on this engagement of youth will have profound implications for the future.

Some congregations and members of congregations, especially in diverse communities, show a commitment to their communities and to meeting needs. Many new ideas and forms are "bubbling up" to tackle and solve problems. If we can discover ways to marry such local congregational passion and the capacity of some of our larger SMOs, people would benefit, and their worlds would improve.

While some congregations will not embrace the expression of their ministry within the public arena, SMOs express passion about aligning themselves with those congregations who want to change the world. When we pursue that passion, barriers fall away. It is a matter of alignment in mission.

Future Leadership for Social Ministry Organizations

Finding committed and qualified persons to continue the legacy of the Lutheran commitment to social justice has been a critical question for the whole church. Some of the leaders present at this roundtable discussion demonstrate personally that leaders emerge in different ways and have followed various routes in their journeys.

> "I grew up as a 'pastor's kid' in a bi-racial town," writes Fred Aigner. "My first call to parish ministry provided me the opportunity to serve a congregation that self-consciously understood itself to be a mix of people. The church then mirrored the community's racial mix. In the late '70s and early '80s, I served another parish where I added 'wellness' to my passion for diversity. Then came a call to a growing parish where its deep and abiding commitment to social ministry transformed me. From there Lutheran Social Services of Illinois called me to the position I hold. Overall, the church has been instrumental at every juncture in my formation. I would not have been led to this call had I not been nourished and shaped by our church's commitment to our broken world, for which God in his love gave his Son."

For Sam Sipes, the route to Lutheran social ministry leadership was quite different.

> I have spent my entire adult life working in social services. At the age of eighteen, I worked as a community organizer. While in college, I worked as a direct care worker in residential treatment. I have worked as a social worker in a community mental health center, an administrator of an assisted living facility, a multisite program manager, and an agency leader.
>
> Social work was my occupation before social ministry was my vocation. I was not raised in the church, and I really did not become a practicing Christian until I was in my thirties. I went to work at a Lutheran social ministry agency before I became Lutheran. It was the witness of my colleagues and agency supporters that led me to become Lutheran. I always had a passion for my work, and Lutheran theology helped me recognize that passion as one indication of God's calling.

Roberta Nestaas also began as a social worker. "I have been a CEO in Lutheran social ministry since 1990. I started as a half-time social worker in one of our predecessor agencies in 1977. Since then I served as CEO of two of the predecessor agencies and of the merged one since 2001. In Lutheran social ministry, I believe the CEO is also the spiritual leader of the organization. That has been one of the most humbling and rewarding parts of my work."

Jill Schumann recounts that she was first introduced to the Lutheran church as a child, when her family chose to attend the nearby Lutheran congregation. There she found an exceptional pastor, church music, and an extended church family. Education has also been a significant part of Schumann's development as a leader.

> PhD studies in a Marxist-oriented history department sharpened my faith and my thinking. The good fortune of a predoctoral public health fellowship at the national Center for Alcohol Studies converted me from academic to practitioner. I spent the next years working in the field of addiction treatment and behavioral health as a clinician, administrator, and program developer in both for-profit and nor-for-profit firms. When I was hired by an entrepreneur to build his new business from scratch, I knew that there were skills and administrative systems I needed to acquire quickly. I turned to a social friend, Tom Hurlocker, the CEO of a Lutheran social ministry organization, and asked to be mentored, and I also enrolled in an evening MBA program.

After several years in Lutheran social ministry, Jill came to Lutheran Services in America. "While the Lutheran church has been important throughout my life, the direct intersection of church and career was a forty-something phenomenon for me," she adds.

Organizing for Social Ministry

The significant turning point for Lutheran social ministry was the creation of Lutheran Services in America in the late 1990s. While many of our SMOs started from congregational ministries or from other local community and individual enterprises, Lutheran Services in America now consists of three hundred member organizations and ranks as the top organization in the country in terms of its total budget for delivering services.

This expansive delivery system has demonstrated how the church can serve everyone more effectively when passions, commitments, resources, and expertise come together in an integrated system of care. The relationship of service to advocacy in LSA reflects how people are viewing social issues and social change. Yet there are always challenges to what we have become and what we have learned. On the one hand, some local groups often splinter away from the professional movement. People who start up the "garage sale" version of service delivery are well intentioned but often naïve about the ability to sustain services or about an approach that will actually improve the lives of people. On the other hand, there are highly successful business folks who think that the reason the world's problems are not solved is that nonprofits are being run by nonprofessionals. There are also the "super professionals" who will fund only what they can measure. Against those reservations about who we are and why and how we do what we do, our mission is to pull together a service organization dedicated to high-quality care and to responsible stewardship of resources.

Thirty percent of SMOs operate with budgets under $2.5 million. Many of these are congregationally owned, volunteer driven, and skilled at recruiting volunteers. Whether they can sustain their energy and their service is always an open question. Our history has shown that Lutheran agencies and organizations responded in a variety of ways to maintain Lutheran identity and service, especially when funding became limited in times of economic crisis. Might we be heading toward other configurations in the future, as our predecessors did in the past?

Whether small and large organizations will survive as they are depends on the kinds of services provided. Government support through programs and contracts might determine what forms these ministries take in the future. The question for the church is how to position itself, on the one hand, to provide stability for social service and, on the other hand, to be able to turn on a dime and respond to changing situations.

Funding Social Service

Our ministries, like the ministry of Jesus, always respond to the specific needs of people. In Jesus' time, as in ours, people have complex needs. Most people we serve are "dually diagnosed." People might be poor and emotionally ill, unemployed resident aliens and physically sick. The profound growth and complexity of human need stretches us beyond our resources.

Yet the theology of the cross leads us directly and inevitably to those people in need. "My passion," notes Dave Larson, "is finding a way—creatively and collaboratively—to meet the needs of those we come upon who are hurting on the side of the road."

Funding for our ministries faces challenges. One issue is that in some areas the public is losing its trust of charities. Because of some isolated scandals, many people are suspicious of nonprofit agencies, how nonprofits handle contributions, and the quality of their care. In some parts of the country, the word "Lutheran" in an agency's title might elicit contributions, because service has led to an image of high quality and integrity in circles of influence both within and outside the Lutheran church. In other areas, like Florida and the northwest, many people do not know what "Lutheran" means, and because many congregations are struggling to survive, contributions by Lutheran constituents are not impressive. We need to strengthen our reputation as a worthy recipient of contributions among Baptists, Roman Catholics, and other denominations besides our own.

While only a small percentage of a large SMO budget comes from church units and individuals in congregations, their contributions enhance the ministries in several ways. Contributions enable many organizations to subsidize care for persons who have no other support or who are in programs not covered by government assistance programs (like residents in assisted living units). Contributions also enable organizations to respond to sudden and unexpected needs, as well as provide start-up funds for services that might develop into lasting programs. Further, contributions enable SMOs to leverage the financing of programs and units that are necessary to meet needs.

Contributions from congregations and from the public arena are affected by the national and global economy. The crisis in the subprime market that surfaced in 2007 could affect social ministry organizations in a variety of ways. When people who are holding tax-exempt bonds cannot sell them, funding sources diminish. The energy crisis can send the economy into inflation, and decreased demand for goods brings recession. We can never predict where and when the next challenge to financial resources will occur.

We might be at a turning point that is the reverse of the one our agencies faced in the 1960s. Thanks to government programs at that time, some ministries of our agencies were able to grow beyond imagination. Prior to that point, our organizations relied almost exclusively on private revenue.

Lutheran service agencies learned how to survive at least as well as anybody else, finding creative ways to fund their ministries. We might need to summon that same kind of creativity today. A hopeful sign at the present is that even while ELCA membership is declining, the contributions to the church and its agencies are increasing.

Government contracts that have allowed some agencies to grow have introduced at the same time new challenges: understandably, along with the funding came increased federal and state requirements. These regulations put pressure on the smaller agencies that have difficulty garnering the resources to meet all the requirements. Further, some agencies expanded considerably by directing their ministries toward government contracts, but when the government monies became tight, the contracts ceased. We have shown, over the years, that we can serve people even apart from government funding. In the aftermath of Katrina, for example, we amassed money and armies of volunteers to assist its victims.

Perhaps for the long term we need to develop a revenue base that is quite different from what we know today. Funding for ministries will have to come from many different sources. Finding those revenue sources will determine how we continue to serve people in need.

Our partnerships with government agencies will require of us more advocacy on behalf of the most vulnerable persons in our society, continued expertise in demonstrating the high quality of our service, and our commitment to serve the common good. As the needs of persons become more complex, even multidiagnosed, we will need to change public perceptions about needs and services.

Calling and Hope

The future of Lutheran social services will continue to focus on direct service of needs, advocacy on behalf of the most needy, and education of society and the rest of the church. Those several roles constitute our response to the gospel of Jesus Christ and our dedication to God the Creator. The same gospel calls us to serve as the point of energy that creates the future, "a future with hope" (Jer. 29:11). Now is the opportunity for us to grab hold of that calling. We can harness that energy to serve by our collective capacity in Lutheran Services in America.

Shortly after its founding, LSA's board of directors established policies that outlined the difference this new organization would make—the ends toward which it should focus its energy in its first decade.

1. Being Lutheran in social ministry is identifiable, valued, and supported by social ministry organizations, church bodies, and communities.
2. The Lutheran social ministry system of services is strengthened, enhanced, and better integrated.
3. Lutheran social ministry organizations have the ability to thrive and serve.
4. Lutheran social ministry organizations have an effective voice for service and justice to church, to government, and to society.
5. Lutheran social ministry organizations are valued ministries and valuable partners with the ELCA and LCMS (churchwide, synod/district, congregation) in the work of service, witness, and justice.

As LSA looks forward to the next decade in its ministry, its board has been focusing on the future, even on shaping the future to strengthen and widen the sense of community. Directing its energy under the theme "Called to Love and Serve Our Neighbors," the LSA board of directors adopted five new "ends" early in 2008 (see below).[1]

LSA's Work for the Next Decade: Called to Love and Serve Our Neighbors

Christ's call has compelled and sustained Lutheran social ministry across centuries and continents. Each of the Lutheran health and human service organizations began when a faithful person responded to this call and invited others along on the journey. This call to love and serve our neighbors continues to shape the work of Lutheran Services in America. LSA is called to strengthen Lutheran social ministry organizations and their connections to the church and to one another. And this strong Lutheran system is called to embrace and shape the future with enthusiasm, savvy, and resolve to create communities that are generous, inclusive, and just.

1. LSA and its members, in partnership with others, are leading a movement of hope and grace toward a society that values generosity, inclusion, justice, and mutual care.

"For you were called to freedom . . . but through love become slaves to one another. For the whole law is summed up in a single commandment, 'You shall love your neighbor as yourself'" (Gal. 5:13-14).

From Holy Scriptures and from the life and teachings of Jesus, Christians know the call to love God and to love our neighbors near and far. God's intent is that people will live in harmony, caring for one another. The face of God is mirrored in each person, and everyone is gifted and blessed by the Creator. LSA and its members, along with many others, are called to work toward a vision of community that recognizes the worth of each person in God's eyes and assures that all people can meet their needs and contribute their talents.

LSA and its members resolve to work together so that people can experience the joy of generosity and the increased sense of connection, safety, and freedom that come from knowing that neighbors will care for them, just as they care for their neighbors. The poverty of spirit and deep hunger that status and material wealth cannot solve can be transformed as people glimpse the power of coming together across abilities, generations, races, and the globe. LSA will spread the message of hope, of abundance, of a willingness to tend our common good. LSA will work with others of good will to insist that everyone should be able to live in safety and dignity with the supports they need. There are no illusions that human efforts can make the world perfect, but Christ calls us to love and serve our neighbors nonetheless.

2. Lutheran social ministry expresses a spirit of possibility and a will that shapes the future.

While some people struggle just to react to the rapid changes coming at them, Lutheran social ministry organizations together are shaping the future. With LSA as the catalyst, the strengths and imagination of three hundred organizations will be mobilized to make a difference for individuals and communities. With the goal of ensuring that all people can thrive in and contribute to community, LSA and its members will borrow insights from a wide range of cultures, disciplines, and industries and translate them into new possibilities.

Lutheran organizations will embrace innovation and new ways of working. New technology and social networking will enhance quality of life, independence, and connectedness. New organizational structures, new partnerships, and new ways of understanding relationships will cultivate new fields. Advocacy, organizing, and service will engage a broader base of support when infused with fresh language and ideas. Philanthropy will be energized as new audiences and new tools are employed. Collaboration with corporations, government, foundations, and a host of uncommon partners will mobilize new resources to tackle multidimensional issues. Congregations and social ministry organizations can discover new ways to come together to share the gospel in words and actions.

Lutheran organizations will be leaders in seizing opportunities and solving problems—providing glimpses of the future we envision. This spirit of possibility and resolve stems from an unwavering hope in God, and that has been a hallmark of steadfast and durable Lutheran social ministry organizations across many generations.

3. Lutheran social ministry organizations live out their Lutheran identities.

"Lutheran" is LSA's first name, and LSA is called to reinforce that which binds this alliance together. Each of the more than three hundred Lutheran health and human service organizations is affiliated with the Evangelical Lutheran Church in America (ELCA), is recognized by the Lutheran Church–Missouri Synod (LCMS), or has relationships with both. The Old and New Testaments, Lutheran confessions and theology, Lutheran history, connections to Word and Sacrament ministries, and a commitment to live out a faithful witness to God's love for all people bind the members of LSA together as the body of Christ with a Lutheran accent.

LSA will provide encouragement, opportunities for learning and discussion, resources, and stimuli for its members to understand and live out their Lutheran identities and church connections. It will help to identify and shape leaders who see the work as ministry. It will share partnerships between congregations and LSA member organizations that are working well. It will seek out collaborative relationships with other agencies and institutions of the church. And it will be a faithful alliance partner to all LSA members with integrity and care, honoring differences and seeking understanding.

In this next decade, Lutheran social ministry organizations will ever more fully incorporate the hallmarks of Lutheran understanding into their daily work. LSA members will live out grace, vocation, neighborliness, forgiveness, mercy, and community. Lutheran social ministry will embrace the complexity of the human experience and will build on the gift of Jesus Christ and the gifts God has given each person. Lutheran social ministry will continue to be dynamic and active in the world on behalf of the neighbor—steadfast over time, yet forward thinking.

4. Lutheran social ministry organizations are healthy and vital, engaged in effective service and advocacy.

As part of a larger network, each social ministry organization has the opportunity to give and to receive—everything from knowledge and encouragement to forms and programs. In the midst of expanding and ever-more-complex needs and opportunities, together we will find new efficiencies, new resources, and new pathways to make a difference. Lutheran organizations will be employers of choice; will excel at effective, high-quality services; and will adhere to high standards of transparency and accountability. They will be blessed with board and staff leaders who are highly skilled and who have a passion for ministry. They will have sufficient resources to meet needs and seize opportunities. They will link service and advocacy so that real change happens for individuals, families, and communities.

LSA will work to ensure that its members not only survive but also are able to move into the future healthy and strong. It will take the expertise, creativity, and engagement of everyone to make this happen.

5. The Lutheran social ministry system has integrated, results-driven capacity.

Lutheran Services in America is an alliance of the ELCA, the LCMS, and their three hundred independent social ministry, health, and human service organizations. Each of these organizations has a unique mission, special strengths, valuable expertise, and faithful boards, staffs, and volunteers. Together, they touch the lives of more than one in fifty Americans every year and have operating budgets in excess of $9 billion. Imagine the possibilities as those strengths come together!

Together in LSA, the system will grow more robust and become better integrated. LSA's members will collaborate readily with one another and with others. New technology and new forms of convening offer new ways to learn together, to share strengths, to collaborate, to speak out, to solve problems, and to seize opportunities. The expertise, experience, effectiveness, and power of Lutheran social ministry organizations will be harnessed and connected for greater impact.

LSA commits to making the kind of difference that can only be made together, to building a system that leverages individual strengths for a greater good. That bold picture calls for strong bonds that promote strong social ministry organizations. It calls for strong connections within the Lutheran churches and beyond. It calls for networked capacity and strong collective resolve.

The next decade beckons. The future will be different. The question is, "How will it be different?" Lutheran Services in America is called to strengthen Lutheran social ministry organizations and their connections to the church and to one another. This strong Lutheran system is called to embrace the future with enthusiasm, savvy, and resolve to create communities that are diverse and inclusive and that offer all people the chance to thrive in and contribute to community—to answer God's call to love and serve our neighbors.

Epilogue

Bearing Risk in a Broken World

Martin E. Marty

This essay makes the case for governmental support of our social ministry organizations and agencies as if we were making it directly to legislators and state-based officials. Most of the principles presented here are valid whether the government is intentionally directing its resources away from social programs or itself is undergoing massive debt that challenges its priorities for fiscal responsibility.

Our real audience and readership, we hope, will be the leaders in congregations or the constituencies of our agencies. We hope the case presented here will better inform and inspire them. We also hope it will help them devise instruments or organize forces to make their influence felt in governmental circles, as well as advise them about improving support of the agencies on other than governmental terms.

A Voice of Faith-Based Organizations

Lutheran social ministry organizations were faith-based long before the term "faith-based" entered the vocabulary of the American public. We are happy to identify with the word and to enter into discussion about what it means, should mean, or what it might mean for organizations like ours.

Lutheran social ministries, well represented by Lutheran Services in America and integral to the work of this country, belong to a long tradition. The roots are twenty-five hundred years old, planted in the soil of the Hebrew prophets, in scriptures common to Jews and Christians alike. We do not claim that such texts and traditions belong only to Jews and Christians—Muslims, for example, have elaborate visions and serious practices in the fields of alms-giving and doing works of service—but the biblical language conveys the messages of faith to vast majorities of citizens and even more so to believing communities within them. For two thousand years, Christians, drawing on New Testament language, have found ways specific for their communities to be of service to others.

Behind our Lutheran social services is a five-hundred-year tradition, originally in northern Europe, of applying mandates and accepting promises that coincide with the faith of the Protestant reformers of the sixteenth century. Many of the modern forms of charitable giving and service grew up on this Protestant and particularly Lutheran terrain. All these histories, brought along with immigrants from Europe, now motivate millions of North Americans—and their counterparts around the world. It is that "Lutheran-influenced" world that concerns us here, though we coordinate our work with other Christians, other believers, and other people of good will wherever we are in action.

The threat to continuing our service through massive government debt and drastic cutbacks in financial support for our work is a constant concern. Foreseen and even threatened decreases in funding will drastically jeopardize services rendered to thousands of citizens by our organizations and others—with no one in sight to take up work we would have to abandon.

The Framework for Responsible Action

Lutheran ministry organizations, then, are not newcomers to the field. They are not improvising untried programs to try to sell them to the state in a period when more and more citizens favor our work. They are not trying to "line up at the trough" of taxpayers' funding of ventures that they dream up on the spot to enhance their own organizations. They have been at work in the human services field for many years—with faithfulness and compassion and imagination, meeting specific human needs as they identified them.

As soon as the ancestors of today's supporters reached American shores, or soon after converts identified with Lutheran causes, these pioneers set to work, with their eye on the needs of the diseased, undernourished, ill-housed, aged, parentless, disabled, and members of other categories. They did this with penny-a-week offerings when congregations gathered, and they invented festivals to raise funds for supporting the causes, as did their counterparts in other traditions. Their social ministry involved both individual responses to the gospel and, more singularly, corporate responses by the church.

The framework changed as the population and the needs grew, while the resources of church members dwindled (comparatively). It was in awareness of the way demand for dollars outweighed the availability of dollars that led Lutherans, among others, to look for sources of funds beyond those of their own faithful. This meant addressing philanthropists, foundations, endowments, and companies and corporations, who enlarged their own contributions, something they had to do judiciously because many of these also served other faith communities. Eventually the only entity that could be of help was the government. The legislative representatives of the people made some legal adjustments that enhanced the work. These took the form of tax deductions, the offering and realization of professionals who could tutor and monitor the work of employees and volunteers.

Still, such an approach grossly limited religious organizations' potential to reach minimal levels of needed services. That situation led visionary political figures to propose legally sound and morally popular supplements to churchly dollar contributions. Years ago, devising templates that were widely applicable, Lutheran social ministry organizations carefully looked for and then found ways to put the energies of religious associations to work without compromising the interests of non- or other-believing citizens. This system was worked out some years ago for many organizations and has remained popular and efficient.

In the newer stage, local governments have begun to take advantage of the energies—financial, spiritual, and technical—available to them through these social ministry organizations as a means of enlarging the organizations' work without endangering legally agreeable division of labor among religious and governmental groups. It is that enlarged scope of work that is in jeopardy.

Questions

The first question that people sometimes ask is, If the organizations achieved their purposes and met their goals in the past, why do they need funds from taxpayers now? If those governmental funds decline, cannot these agencies simply return to the way they formerly acted, before there were revenues put to work among them? Among the answers: first, they did not achieve their purposes; they fell far short of their goals. Second, delivery of services has grown much more expensive, because of insurance regulations, increased cost in training employees, decades of inflation, and the breakdown of some other support systems—most notably, for many, the family and neighborhood.

A second question: What about the human cost if there is a decline in agency support? Here we can illustrate amply. We have seen our caseworkers return from their rounds almost spent from what they have seen in the way of human need, almost as demoralized as those who need the services. What caseworkers see is: large numbers of children who need foster care or would welcome adoption; couples who are turned down because there is no way safely to connect them with potential foster or adopted children; seniors in a culture where life expectancy continues to grow faster than funds to support the lives of the aged can rise to meet them. People denied medical care because they lack the means to have insurance suffer when caseworkers are not able to advocate for them, deliver them to medical institutions, or help them resume life beyond such institutions.

We have seen no data that suggest that these needs of unfortunate citizens can be met if funds are cut back on our organizational front. We also have seen no data to suggest that other, more efficient and effective means of relating to publics would be available if tax support of our agencies diminishes.

A third question: Are not our organizations now suffering from having gotten into the habit of being dependent upon government, of being too ready to be deliverers of services that the state needs and hence supports? No, we have been well aware of sayings warning against dependency: "whoever takes the king's shekels gets the king's shackles" (in the form of do's and don'ts that limit and restrict their work). We are glad to "open the books" for people to see how much of our energy has gone into sustaining independent religious motivations. In some senses, we suffer from our success: we have learned to serve far more people in far better ways than our grandparents could. Unfortunately, however, the needs in society have grown. Fortunately, thanks to mass media and the like, we are better informed about how our clients and potential clients live than our ancestors could be before cameras, radio, television, and the like made those in need more visible and thus more urgent for our consciences.

EFFICIENCY IN OUR ORGANIZATIONS

The more delivery of services can be backed by volunteer and lay support, the more taxpayers will save. It happens that religious believers are motivated to keep in their line of vision the easily overlooked numbers of fellow citizens who need their aid. It further happens that to some extent these believers, gathered in congregations or support groups, provide direct aid. Urban churches come first to the aid of people in crime-ridden neighborhoods; rural church members have taken up offerings, harvested and brought food, or held quilting bees and sewing events to support their neighbors in need. Yet at their best, all these efforts fell far short of what ought to have been done. Goods are necessary for sustenance; services are needed for making living more bearable and increasing opportunities.

Change, meanwhile, came to these supporting congregations and agencies. Population changes—the fact that the inherited practices connected with charity are interrupted when people move away, as they do in farm country, the suburbs, and the city alike—present one set of problems. The exciting increase in the freedom of women to add work outside the home to work inside the home has meant that many of them had to cut down their volunteer hours—and women have historically been the majority of social ministry volunteers. Economic change (the two-income family necessity) makes it difficult for many people to give and to serve. Despite these changes, these congregants have made significant adjustments, and have continued to serve their neighbors, often under difficult circumstances.

"FAITH-BASED" IN THE NEW SETTING

We have come to the point where much of our work leaves us no choice but to seek government funds, although we have done this seeking following careful guidelines. Secular service agencies that have not depended upon the loyalty of religious congregants through the decades certainly cannot enter the zone with new energies and funds: they have suffered decline in voluntary support and must make appeals to many of the same sources that religious agencies do. Studies show that loyalties to such secular agencies are more likely to wear thin as generations pass and people move; the significant minorities who stay put, and get to know their neighbors and neighborhood, the state of their state, and the landscape of supporters are more likely to show loyalty, which most often occurs through religious motivations and institutions.

There is no foreseeable way to enhance the private funding sector in any quantum-leap manner. Yes, in a utopia, religious supporters would tithe, and then double and triple tithe, at expense to their retirement funds, their children's college funds, the somewhat luxurious items and experiences that they welcome. Yes, if the religious messages motivated the whole range of the memberships to take dramatic risks and forego luxuries, more needs could be met. In an ideal world, the depth of sacrifice to which our messages point should produce more funds. Yet in many cases and places, we have exhausted leaders and not completely motivated followers among volunteers and givers.

Our organizations take great pains to band people together on the assumption that educating and inspiring them about needs and techniques for addressing needs will increase the cohort of supporters and the amount of support. There are fund drives, retreats, media exposures, fairs, presentations at religious gatherings, and fieldwork and involvement by the young who are being trained to be mature service providers. The organizations cannot continue that practice if all of their declining funds go directly to those needing care, helpless children and the aged alike. Training people for service and making cases and situations of need visible go on with special fervor and finesse among voluntary religious agencies.

The Renewal of Generosity and the Increase in Risk

In the past, when the Ladies' Aid and the Men's Club assessed need in and at the edges of congregations, it was easy for them to be good stewards and to retain low-risk control of church charities. While the activities at such times and places truly addressed profound needs when there was not yet any kind of government safety net, the operations were also relatively tidy. Funding amounts were so low that it was not hard to account for them. There was often a kind of "respectability" among those served. In the living memory of leaders in our congregations and agencies are the incidents when, once a year, there would be an "orphan's festival," with a visit to orphanages. There visitors would toss dimes on the blankets of children's beds, seeing that as a way of making their lives more endurable until other congregation members would come along to replace the parents who had been killed in accidents or lost in epidemics. Providing counseling meant supporting a pastor to spend hours with a member couple in marital trouble.

It was shocking and sometimes offended givers when the risk of dealing with the unrespectable was added to this work. It was hard for them to cope with the fact that most child care was not directed to orphans but to children of unmarried mothers, that much of what they suffered came from abuses perpetrated by mothers' boyfriends, that couples in need of counsel had also been involved with abuse and were usually not married. The outcome of counsel, service, or aid involved risk because so many of the people served had to return themselves to situations of risk. The growth in government funding in some ways lowered the risk, since there was now greater potential for follow-through. But other risks have risen, among them presently the risk of losing so much revenue support that our programs will be mere skeletons—as, figuratively and sometimes close to literally, might some of our clients, the hungry, the ill–cared for.

Against all the depressing features of contemporary culture, it is also possible to talk of an increase in generosity. We have seen the development of attention to human rights, therapies, educational changes that draw more people into their orbits, moderate welfare reforms that at best protect those who cannot become able self-supporters, while turning others into agents of their own fortunes. And through it all, thanks to vital congregations, professional motivating staffs, and visions of need presented by mass media, many in the public have seen their hearts stirred. They build houses for Habitat for Humanity. Their teens go on spring-vacation labor endeavors in Appalachia or the inner city. Long-retired people put talents and skills to work that in a previous generation would not have been available or sought.

Yet all these signs and signals, these warrants and promises, will be executed within narrow walls and under low ceilings if funding is drastically cut back. So we shall be asking those who believe as we do, who are in communion and community with us, to take risks: they will be bidden to acquire skills to go along with informed consciences, increased clarity of vision, and theological refreshing about how in government, as in religious life, we are somehow "members one of another." They will be asked to take risks in their imaginations, finding ways to present cases, create publicity, and make friends among people of influence who can alter the dangerous course that seems to lie ahead. It is easier to undertake no risk, to sit at home hoping someone else makes the case and provides the bodies and voices. That "someone else" is likely to be someone awakened to risk taking, someone in the family or down the pew or next door or in the next parish.

Speaking up Lutheranly

To this point we have deliberately restrained ourselves from zeroing in and making the case in specifically Lutheran terms and with Lutheran understandings. We did that not out of a fear of risk taking, though we recognize that formal theological terms can be offensive in the public sphere. Instead, we aimed to provide a kind of generic outline, using the language of the state and voluntary agencies. Robert Booth Fowler has said that in a pluralistic society such as ours, people of profound motivation and specific outlooks often have to "hold back," almost bite their tongues, chomp at the bit, knowing that they could go deeper, say more, and achieve much more by drawing on the stories, language, memories, and intentions of specific communities.

So, let's be frank. In public perceptions and usually as a result of self-examination, Lutherans turn out to be better at mercy than justice—that is, at expressing love rather than promoting justice. Today we are called to engage in "justice-seeking neighbor love," as Cynthia Moe-Lobeda puts it. Love is easier to talk about because we hear and know that God is love (though love is not God), that whoever claims to love God but does not love the neighbor is living a lie, that the Christian gospel lets us love rather than forces us to love. Justice is complicated because in a political world (we are not speaking here of political parties in any direct sense), the *polis*, the human city, brings people of many commitments together. It is difficult to effect justice without taking risks, stepping on toes, bumping into the interests of others—some of whom may sometimes be right when we are not!—organizing, and dividing.

When we do the works of justice, some Lutherans know and say that there are risks to the gospel, the good news of what God does for us through grace in Christ. They know long histories wherein Christians learned that if they did charitable work and achieved just goals, they would get better places in heaven, would know rewards. They gave alms in a kind of transaction with God, a "calculus." The Lutheran Reformation opposed such transactions and asked believers not to set out to impress God with the works of justice but to "make faith active in love." Our agencies, organizations, charitable groups, and works are dedicated to that endeavor and goal, and no one dares to risk violating it.

That does not leave us off the justice hook, free to take no risks. Isaiah 58, among hundreds of other texts is in our canon, reminds us that fasting and being pious is not the kind of response for which God asks. Such Bible passages give notices and assignments that provide some substance for welfare legislation and agendas for our agencies: to serve those who "loose the bonds of injustice," to "undo the thongs of the yoke," to risk letting "the oppressed go free," to "share our bread with the hungry," to "bring the homeless poor into our houses," to "cover the naked"—and yes, to take care of our own kin! (Justice and mercy also begin at home; they do not just stay there!)

Isaiah does not describe the means by which that work goes on. The text does not commit us to being Republican or Democrat, left or right, overreliant on government or overreliant on "the private sector." Each generation needs to find its own way to effect God's "justice-seeking neighbor love" through us. Today variations on faith-based activities offer some means. Doing so does not give us license to be exclusivist, to take our distinctive gospel message and argue that no one who does not share it can serve human purpose. We even believe that they can serve divine purpose, as the writings of Martin Luther and preachers in his train have reminded us in biblical terms for centuries. It does not mean that we will use the same language when dealing with publics that we use in gathered communions and communities. But we do believe that the language of "justice-seeking neighbor love" can be translated so other-believers and non-believers will understand what we are about and come to support it, regarding us a partner in faith-based endeavors that they approach in other ways than we do.

Let us suppose, as we take these risks, we offend some low-risk or other-risking fellow congregants and believers or "outsiders." Christians are called to be ready to give offense in the name of Jesus, who says those are blessed who do not take offense at him. The offending can take the form of friendly challenges: Dear fellow believers, if you think these agencies and their alliances are not the best or even the appropriate way to fulfill divine commands or spread the works of love, what equivalents do you propose? Or shall neither of us come up with a plan or program? Shall we be at the mercy of our own apathy and timidity and lack of venturesomeness? Are not our fellowships strong enough that they can call forth patience with each other as we take risks?

We are doing this not to turn "retro" and adopt the styles—effective though many of them were—of the social activists of decades ago. We are doing this to look ahead and adopt the styles of God's servants who engage in action in society, in the social sphere, always grounding our work in the divine message.

Lutherans are careful to distinguish between the divine law and the gospel. Through the law God effects justice and righteousness, not salvation. Through the gospel, believers in faith are given gifts that make them "right with God" and free for the other. The gospel is the power of God "unto salvation." The law, which is expressive of God's justice, is the power of God "unto the care of the neighbor."

We do not believe that people can be *coerced* into charitable, philanthropic, justice-seeking activity. They cannot be *moralized* into it, as believers. Moralism is as weak an instrument as coercion is contradictory. Christians cannot be *seduced* or *beguiled* into serving God in the neighbor. They are moved by *story*, the story of a Creator God who provides the good things people are to receive through the means of justice also provided by God. They are moved by the story of God's giving of God's self in Jesus, the crucified and risen Lord. They are moved by the stories of Jesus being generous, discerning, and able to motivate, by stories of Publicans and Good Samaritans, and saintly believers in all ages—including our own.

Where does that leave the Christian who has strong evangelistic impulses? We would like to think that all Christians have such. At the same time, they have to take the risk of not playing God in all human interactions, forcing people to hear a message on all occasions, acting as if God is a God of prey who pounces and takes advantage of people in their weakness. Someone has said that in the parable Jesus called the Samaritan (outsider) "good" because he provided oil and wine and coin and care—without taking advantage of a victim who was "strapped to his ass" and handing him a tract or preaching a sermon. Evangelization is born of the impulse to see the works of Christ's love reach as far as possible and to be seconded with story wherever appropriate. The returns are in, through the ages: where God is well served with "justice-seeking neighbor love," there the message of the gospel spreads, and people respond in freedom and with integrity.

Conflicts, Partnerships, and Vision

We are all too familiar with the history of conflict between Christians and all those who are not part of our circle of believers or agencies that are not born of Christian impulses, including the government. Of course, this side of eternity, there must be and will always be distinctions, separations, and tensions between our faith community and other communities. We know that "principalities and powers" have their domain this side of eternity. Yet the God who could call Cyrus, king of Persia, "his anointed" (Isa. 45:1) and "my shepherd" (Isa. 44:28) even though Cyrus did not know God's name or serve God consciously, gives risk-taking believers and communities freedom to find ways to work with government, secular partners, and others—without loss of integrity.

Even among partners, our faith drives us toward challenge and confrontation. Now that we have progressively learned how to partner in faith-based ventures, we must confront governmental agencies and lawmakers, winsomely but clearly, so that meeting the needs of the vulnerable rises to priority. We know that inside history we remain broken, our institutions are transient, our endeavors finite, our motives mixed. Yet in the midst of that brokenness, there is always the vision of *shalom,* a vision partly realized whenever God's suffering children find care and solace—and justice.

Notes

1. The Identity and Work of God

1. Some of the details result simply from the ways stories developed in the early church. The "woman" in Matthew and Mark becomes identified as Mary, the sister of Lazarus and Martha, in John's Gospel. The location of the incident moves from the home of Simon the leper in Matthew and Mark to the home of Mary and Martha in John. The woman anointed Jesus' head in Matthew and Mark, while in John (and in Luke's version of the anointing incident) Mary anointed Jesus' feet and wiped them with her hair. The indignation arises from "some" in Mark, from "the disciples" in Matthew, and from "Judas" in John. For a discussion about these tendencies in the Gospel stories, see Rudolf Bultmann, *History of the Synoptic Tradition*, 2nd ed., trans. John Marsh (New York: Harper & Row, 1968), 64–68, 263, 276–77.

2. Luke eliminated the entire quotation from his Gospel and moved the event about the anointing woman out of the Passion story. He reset the incident to precede a list of women who became disciples. The anointing of Jesus' feet by a woman known as "a sinner" became a story of forgiveness (Luke 7:36-50). Did Luke think that Jesus' saying detracted from his Gospel's focus on the poor?

3. For a thorough discussion of the terms in Greek and Hebrew, see πτωχός in *Theological Dictionary of the New Testament*, ed. Gerhard Kittel (Grand Rapids: Eerdmans, 1968), 6:885–915.

4. For a fuller discussion of the nature of poverty and its causes, see Walter E. Pilgrim, *Good News to the Poor: Wealth and Poverty in Luke-Acts* (Minneapolis: Augsburg Publishing House, 1981), 39–46.

5. Ibid., 73–74.

6. Bruce J. Malina, *The New Testament World: Insights from Cultural Anthropology* (Atlanta: John Knox, 1981), 84–88.

7. Admittedly, the author of Luke-Acts and the writer of the Epistle of James set as opposites the rich and the poor (see Luke 1:53; James 1:9). Those writers, we shall see, intend to express how difficult it is for the rich to trust solely in God and the failure of the rich to use wealth to ease the burdens of the poor.

8. Eberhard S. Gerstenberger and Wolfgang Schrage, *Suffering*, trans. John E. Steely (Nashville: Abingdon, 1980).

9. For a discussion of images and counter-images of God in relation to the poor, see Robert Kysar, *Called to Care: Biblical Images for Social Ministry* (Minneapolis: Fortress Press, 1991), 7–29.

10. Gerhard Von Rad, *Old Testament Theology*, trans. D. M. G. Stalker (New York: Harper, 1962), 1:370–83.

11. Klaus Koch, *The Prophets: The Assyrian Period* (Philadelphia: Fortress Press, 1983), 56–62.

12. Luther used this same rationale in his explanation of the commandment against stealing. See the Large Catechism in *The Book of Concord: The Confessions of the Evangelical Lutheran Church*, ed. Robert Kolb and Timothy J. Wengert (Minneapolis: Fortress Press, 2000), 419, lines 246–47.

13. Because eleven commandments appear in Exod. 20:2-17, Judaism and Christian denominations differ on which ten should make the list. By one accounting, the chosen ten amount to five pairs or categories: (1) the person of God (no other gods, no images), (2) what belongs to God (name, Sabbath), (3) family life (parents, no adultery), (4) the free life of the neighbor (no killing, no stealing/kidnapping), and (5) what belongs to the neighbor (no false testimony in court, no coveting). See Hartmut Gese, "The Structure of the Decalogue," *Fourth World Congress of Jewish Studies: Papers*, vol. 1 (1967).

14. James B. Pritchard, ed., *Ancient Near Eastern Texts Relating to the Old Testament*, 2nd ed. (Princeton: Princeton University Press, 1955), 164.

15. They knew also that Elisha repeated the same miracle for the only son of the wealthy Shunammite woman who had provided him hospitality (2 Kings 4:32-37).

16. Eduard Schweizer, *The Good News according to Matthew*, trans. David Green (Atlanta: John Knox, 1975), 79–98.

17. For a fine discussion of the pertinent passages in Acts, see Pilgrim, *Good News to the Poor*, 147–59.

18. John Reumann, *Righteousness in the New Testament* (Philadelphia: Fortress Press, 1982).

19. Ernst Käsemann, *Commentary on Romans*, trans. Geoffrey W. Bromiley (Grand Rapids: Eerdmans, 1980), 323.

20. See Jouette M. Bassler, *God and Mammon: Asking for Money in the New Testament* (Nashville: Abingdon, 1991).

2. The Relief of the Needy in Their Distress

1. *The Works of Josephus*, trans. William Whiston (Peabody, Mass.: Hendrickson, 1987), 528.

2. Rodney Stark, *The Rise of Christianity: How the Obscure, Marginal Jesus Movement Became the Dominant Religious Force in the Western World in a Few Centuries* (San Francisco: HarperSanFrancisco, 1997), 211. Clearly, the ancient Mediterranean world was filled with stories about gods and goddesses who took human form in order to be seen by humans. Yet the story of a god or goddess who would abandon their powers and take human form to *serve humanity unto death* is difficult to find.

3. Ibid., 212.

4. I make the distinction between the historical Paul, who is credited by scholars with writing seven letters, and the anonymous authors of other letters in the New Testament who claimed Pauline authorship. The distinction between the two enables

the reader of the letters to understand better the apparent contradictions between them (for example, praising women as leaders in the authentic letters and ordering them to be silent and submissive in the deutero-Pauline letters).

5. See Wayne A. Meeks, "The Grammar of Christian Practice," in *The Origins of Christian Morality: The First Two Centuries* (New Haven: Yale University Press, 1993), 91–110. While I focus briefly here on texts of the historical Paul (in contrast to those of other writers who used his name), it is important to note that the early Christian experience reflected in the Pauline corpus was only one and perhaps a small slice of that experience. Many other forms of Christianity emerged rather quickly in the first century. Limits of space preclude a more exhaustive analysis of the diverse ways in which these many other Christian communities responded to or even overlooked real human need.

6. Jérôme Carcopino, *Daily Life in Ancient Rome: The People and the City at the Height of the Empire*, ed. Henry T. Rowell, trans. E. O. Lorimer (New Haven: Yale University Press, 1992).

7. *Early Christian Fathers*, ed. and trans. Cyril Richardson (New York: Macmillan, 1970), 287, with emendations.

8. Luke 24:13-35, in which the risen Lord comes to two disciples and forms a small community, interprets the scriptures regarding himself, and breaks bread at table, from whence they leave to enter the city. I would claim that the Lucan text holds both a *memory* of the table fellowship of this historical Jesus and an *instruction* as to where Luke's readers will encounter his presence in their own time: in the community, the scriptures, and the breaking of the bread.

9. Gordon Lathrop, *Holy Things: A Liturgical Theology* (Minneapolis: Fortress Press, 1993), 45–46.

10. Dionysius of Alexander as quoted by Eusebius of Caesarea in his *Church History*, trans. Arthur C. McGiffert, Nicene and Post-Nicene Fathers Series 2 (Grand Rapids: Eerdmans, 1965), 1:307. The reader should keep in mind that Dionysius's report was written at a time when Christians were viewed with either skepticism or hostility in the empire; he wants to hold Christians in a positive light. At the same time, there is evidence to suggest that priests of the Roman deities did little to respond to plague victims.

11. Cyprian of Carthage, *On Mortality*, trans. Ernest Wallis, *Ante-Nicene Fathers* (Grand Rapids: Eerdmans, 1958), 5:473.

12. Tertullian, *Apology*, trans. S. Thelwall, Ante-Nicene Fathers (Grand Rapids: Eerdmans, 1958), 4:47.

13. Aristides, *Apology*, in *A New Eusebius*, ed. J. Stevenson (London: SPCK, 1957), 57–58.

14. See R. A. Markus, *Gregory the Great and His World* (Cambridge: Cambridge University Press, 1997), 112–24.

15. Gregory the Great, *Dialogues*, Book II.

16. The various reforms of Western monasticism were rooted in the desire to "return" to the simplicity of life envisioned in the Rule, a simplicity and equality that could be obscured by the intrusion of cultural values into monastic life.

17. *The Rule of St. Benedict*, ed. Timothy Fry, O.S.B. (Collegeville, Minn.: Liturgical, 1982), 73.

18. Ibid., 27.

19. Contemporary scholars suggest that Gregory portrayed Benedict as a prophetic figure who provided food, drink, and healing in order to underscore Gregory's

conviction that, in the midst of war and deprivation, God continued to act through and for God's people.

20. The cartoon can be found in my *Luther and the Hungry Poor: Gathered Fragments* (Minneapolis: Fortress Press, 2008), 20.

21. Leonardo Boff, *Francis of Assisi: A Model for Human Liberation*, trans. John Diercksmeier (Maryknoll, N.Y.: Orbis Books, 2006), 43–71.

22. Carter Lindberg, *Beyond Charity: Reformation Initiatives for the Poor* (Minneapolis: Fortress Press, 1993), 17–67.

23. Lester Little, *Religious Poverty and the Profit Economy in Medieval Europe* (Ithaca: Cornell University Press, 1978), 97–170.

3. No Greater Service to God than Christian Love

1. *Luther's Works*, American ed., 55 vols. (St. Louis: Concordia; Philadelphia: Fortress Press, 1955–86), 12:311. Hereafter cited as LW.

2. Ibid., 35:365–79.

3. Ibid., 31:327–77.

4. See Matti Jäveläinen, *Gemeinschaft in der Liebe: Diakonie als Lebens- und Wesensäusserung der Kirche im Verständnis Paul Philippis: Mit der Abschiedsvorlesung Philippis "Über die soziale Dimension lutherischer Ekklesiologie"* (Heidelberg: Diakoniewissenschaftliches Institut, 1993).

5. LW 35:45–73, 75–111.

6. Ibid., 35:58, 67.

7. Ibid., 35:50–51.

8. Ibid., 35:51–52.

9. Järveläinen, *Gemeinschaft in der Liebe*, 83.

10. LW 35:57; see also 35:96.

11. Ibid., 35:95; see also "The Babylonian Captivity of the Church" in LW (1520), 36:53.

12. Ibid., 35:98–99.

13. Ibid., 36:46.

14. Ibid., 45:172.

15. Paul Rorem, "The End of All Offertory Processions," *Dialog* 35, no. 4 (1996): 247–50, here 249. On vocation as worship in the realm of the world, see Vilmos Vajta, *Luther on Worship* (Philadelphia: Muhlenberg, 1958).

16. "The Sacrament of the Body and Blood of Christ—Against the Fanatics" (1526), in LW 36:352–53.

17. Larissa Taylor, *Soldiers of Christ: Preaching in Late Medieval and Reformation France* (New York: Oxford University Press, 1992), 150.

18. Juan Luis Vives, *De Subventione Pauperum sive De Humanis Necessitatibus*, ed. C. Mattheeusen and C. Fantazzi (Leiden: Brill, 2002), 143.

19. LW 30:278.

20. Ibid., 2:327, 331; 28:370–72; 30:248.

21. Ibid., 45:233–310.

22. Ibid., 45:159–94.

23. Ibid., 44:213, 189ff.

24. Ibid., 9:147–48; cf. 45:161.

25. Ibid., 44:21–114.

26. *Luthers Werke: Kritische Gesamtausgabe [Schriften]*, 65 vols. (Weimar: H. Böhlau, 1883–1993), 51:325–424. Hereafter cited as WA.

27. See LW 9:139n7.

28. See Jimmy Carter, *Our Endangered Values: America's Moral Crisis* (New York: Simon & Schuster, 2005).

29. Barbara Ehrenreich, *Nickel and Dimed: On (Not) Getting By in America* (New York: Holt, 2002), 221. See also Katherine Newman and Victor Tan Chen, *The Missing Class: Portraits of the Near Poor in America* (Boston: Beacon, 2007).

30. WA 51:396.12–397.3.

31. See "Trade and Usury," in LW 45:231–310.

32. WA 51:417.11–17.

33. LW 21:180; 25:172.

34. WA 51:367.10–368.16.

35. Ibid., 51:325.

36. *Luthers Werke: Kritische Gesamtausgabe: Briefwechsel*, 18 vols. (Weimar: H. Böhlau, 1930–85), 8:403–5. Hereafter cited as WABr.

37. Wolfgang Palaver, "Challenging Capitalism as Religion: Hans G. Ulrich's Theological and Ethical Reflections on the Economy," *Studies in Christian Ethics* 20, no. 2 (2007): 215–30, here 217. Hans G. Ulrich's *Wie Geschöpfe Leben: Konturen evangelischer Ethik* (Münster: Lit Verlag, 2005) discusses Luther and economics.

38. LW 44:213.

39. See Ulrich Duchrow, *Global Economy: A Confessional Issue for the Churches?* (Geneva: WCC Publications, 1987), and Carter, *Our Endangered Values*, 197.

40. LW 9:243.

41. Ibid., 21:183.

42. Ibid., 44:107.

43. WA 51:422.15–423.2.

44. WABr 3:485–86.

45. WA 27:417–18.

46. Ibid., 51:325, 332–36.

47. Ibid., 51:353.29–31.

48. Ibid., 51:354.28.

49. Ibid., 28:360–61.

50. Heiko A. Oberman, "Teufelsdreck: Eschatology and Scatology in the 'Old' Luther," in *The Impact of the Reformation: Essays* (Grand Rapids: Eerdmans, 1994), 62.

51. Doug Marlette, *Shred This Book! The Scandalous Cartoons of Doug Marlette* (Atlanta: Peachtree, 1988), 156.

52. WA 28:360–61.

53. *The Book of Concord: The Confessions of the Evangelical Lutheran Church*, ed. Robert Kolb and Timothy J. Wengert (Minneapolis: Fortress Press, 2000), 31n8.

54. LW 28:256.

55. Ibid., 13, 49.

56. Ibid., 13, 50.

57. Ibid.

58. Ibid., 13, 51.

59. "IRS Audits Church for Anti-War Sermon," OMB Watch, November 15, 2005, http://www.ombwatch.org/article/articleview/3167/1/48?TopicID=1.

4. FAITH ACTIVE IN LOVE

1. For more on Orthodoxy and Pietism, see Eric W. Gritsch, *A History of Lutheranism* (Minneapolis: Fortress Press, 2002), chapters 4–5. Material from chapters 4–6 of *A History of Lutheranism* has been adapted for use in this essay.

2. Quoted in Johannes Wallmann, *Der Pietismus: Die Kirche und ihre Geschichte: Ein Handbuch*, ed. B. Moeller (Göttingen: Vandenhoeck & Ruprecht, 1990), 8; my translation.

3. Philip Jacob Spener, *Pia Desideria*, ed. and trans. Theodore G. Tappert (Philadelphia: Fortress Press, 1964), 92.

4. For details on Francke's life and work, see Wallmann, *Der Pietismus,* chapter 4. A brief description of the school is in *Pietists: Selected Writings*, ed. Peter C. Erb and Theodore G. Tappert (New York: Paulist, 1983).

5. The volumes have been edited by F. De Boor, *Die paränetischen und methodischen Vorlesungen A. H. Franckes*, 2 vols. (Halle: Theologische Habilitation, 1968), and summarized by the same author in *Zeitschrift für Religions und Geistesgeschichte* 20 (1968): 300–320.

6. Wallmann, *Der Pietismus*, 70.

7. Adam Smith, *An Inquiry into the Nature and Causes of the Wealth of Nations,* Great Books of the Western World 39 (Chicago: Encyclopedia Britannica, 1955); Karl Marx, *Capital, Communist Manifesto, and Other Writings,* ed. Max Eastmann (New York: Modern Library, 1932).

8. See G. Everett Arden, *Four Northern Lights: Men Who Shaped Scandinavian Churches* (Minneapolis: Augsburg Publishing House, 1964), for sketches of Grundtvig, Hauge, Rosenius, and Ruotsalainen.

9. See Andreas Aarflot, *Hans Nielsen Hauge: His Life and Message* (Minneapolis: Augsburg Publishing House, 1979). See also Hauge's *Autobiographical Writings*, trans. J. M. Njus (Minneapolis: Augsburg Publishing House, 1954).

10. See *Norwegen, Kirchengeschichte* in *Die Religion in Geschichte und Gegenwart: Handwörterbuch für Theologie und Religionswissenschaft*, 7 vols., 3rd ed. (Tübingen: Mohr, 1957–65), 4:1526. Hereafter cited as RGG.

11. See Wilhelm Löhe, *Three Books about the Church*, ed. and trans. James E. Schaaf (Philadelphia: Fortress Press, 1969), with an introduction to his life and work.

12. See *Fliedner, Theodor* in RGG 2:979 (statistics there). See the summary of his life and work in Abdel R. Wentz, *Fliedner the Faithful* (Philadelphia: Board of Publications of the Lutheran Church in America, 1936). Florence Nightingale (1820–1910), the English pioneer of hospital nursing and battlefield care for the wounded, resided in the Kaiserswerth mother house for a period in 1851.

13. Sketch of the movement in Karl Kupisch, *Deutschland im 19. und 20. Jahrhundert: Ein Handbuch: Die Kirche in ihrer Geschichte*, ed. Kurt D. Schmidt and Ernst Wolf (Göttingen: Vandenhoeck & Ruprecht, 1966), 67–71. See also the detailed study by Friedrich Mahling, *Die innere Mission*, 2 vols. (Gütersloh: Bertelsmann, 1937).

14. See Martin Gerhardt, *Johann Hinrich Wichern*, 3 vols. (Hamburg: Agentur des Rauhen Hauses, 1927–31), and Gerald Christianson, "J. H. Wichern and the Rise of Lutheran Social Institutions," *Lutheran Quarterly* 19 (1967): 357–70.

15. Kupisch, *Deutschland im 19. und 20. Jahrhundert*, 68.

16. See *Stadtmission* in RGG 6:322–24.

17. See *Innere Mission* in RGG 3:759.

18. See Margaret Bradfield, *The Great Samaritan: The Life and Work of Friedrich von Bodelschwingh* (London: Marshall, Morgan & Scott, 1964). Collected works in *Friedrich Bodelschwingh: Ausgewählte Schriften*, ed. Alfred Adam, 2 vols. (Bethel: Bethel Verlag, 1958–64).

19. Blumhardt became world famous through his exorcisms of demons, which he viewed as causes of mental illness. His blow-by-blow account of treating a woman named Gotliebin Dittus became a media event. See the biography by Friedrich Seebass, *Johann Christoph Blumhardt* (Hamburg, 1949).

20. See *Bodelschwingh, Friedrich*, in RGG 1:1336.

21. See *Innere Mission* in RGG 3:762–63.

22. Quotation in *Theologische Realenzyklopädie*, ed. G. Krause and G. Müller, 31 vols. (Berlin: de Gruyter, 1977–2005), 16:170.

23. See *Innere Mission* in ibid., 16:169–70.

24. See *Stoecker, Adolf*, in RGG 6:387.

5. A Sign of God's Grace, A Fruit of Faith

1. Carl Schurz (1829–1906) immigrated to this country and became a spokesman for German immigrants. Supporting Abraham Lincoln's presidential campaign, he was rewarded with the post of ambassador to Spain. During the Civil War he commanded Union troops as a general. In 1869 he was elected senator from Missouri, and in 1877 he was appointed U.S. Secretary of the Interior.

2. David J. Rothman, quoted in *Newsweek*, December 12, 1994. Rothman is Bernard Schoenberg Professor of Social Medicine and History at Columbia University; his books have explored the history of prisons and mental hospitals and the impact of bioethics and law on medicine. He has recently been named president of the Institute on Medicine as a Profession.

3. E. Clifford Nelson, ed., with Theodore G. Tappert, H. George Anderson, August R. Suelflow, Eugene L. Fevold, and Fred W. Meuser, *The Lutherans in North America* (Philadelphia: Fortress Press, 1975), 386. See also E. Theodore Bachman, ed., *Churches and Social Welfare* (New York: National Council of Churches, 1955), 132–33.

4. In June 1839, a free African American, Daniel Payne, who had prepared for the ministry at the Lutheran Seminary at Gettysburg, delivered the oration, on the occasion of his ordination by the Franckean Synod, in support of a report advocating the end of slavery. In 1863, he became president of Wilberforce University in Ohio, the first African American to head a college.

5. J. F. Ohl, *The Inner Mission: A Handbook for Christian Workers* (Philadelphia: General Council Publication House, 1911), 68.

6. "The Great War of Germany against Europe," *Lutheran Church Review* (October 1914), cited by Fred W. Meuser in *Lutherans in North America*, 396.

7. Nelson, *Lutherans in America*, 396–99.

8. J. A. S. Grenville, *A History of the World in the Twentieth Century* (Cambridge: Belknap Press of Harvard University Press, 1994), 127, 132, 136, 147, 148, 150, 164, 175ff., 178, 250, 278, 292, 304.

9. Anthony also campaigned for the abolition of slavery, women's rights to their own property and earnings, and women's labor organizations.

10. By the end of the century this number had climbed to almost twenty thousand.

11. "President's Message," *National Lutheran Council in America Annual Report for 1942*, cited by Nelson, *Lutherans in North America*, 474.

12. Eventually this modest beginning grew into Lutheran World Action, which by 1965 had raised almost $80 million and assisted people in seventy-five countries. The effort was joined by the Board of World Relief of the Lutheran Church–Missouri Synod.

13. F. Dean Leuking, *A Century of Caring, 1868–1968* (St. Louis: Board of Social Ministry, Lutheran Church–Missouri Synod, 1968), 59–63.

14. Ibid., 50.

15. "Report of Representatives to an Intersynodical Lutheran Conference," January 20, 1941, Columbus, Ohio, J. K. Jensen Papers, Northwestern Lutheran Seminary Library, St. Paul, Minnesota, 117–19, cited by Nelson, *Lutherans in North America*.

16. And half of the nation's 1,600 orphanages were church affiliated. See J. Russell Hale, *Touching Lives through Service: The History of Tressler Lutheran Services 1868–1994* (Mechanicsburg, Pa.: Tressler Lutheran Services, 1994), 87.

17. Ibid., 77. The quotations come from the report given to the National Lutheran Council by Dr. Paulssen in 1941.

6. Bringing Hope and Life

1. The author is indebted to the following individuals for their time as well as their patience and understanding, and most especially for the wealth of information they provided regarding Lutheran social ministry: Gayle Adelsman, former director of public relations, Lutheran Social Services of Minnesota; Richard Anderson, director of adoption, Lutheran Social Services of Minnesota; Ralston Deffenbaugh, president and CEO, Lutheran Immigration and Refugee Service; Dr. David Geske, president and CEO, Bethesda Lutheran Home and Services; Gail Hagen, former director, Services to People with Special Needs, Lutheran Social Services of Wisconsin and Upper Michigan; the Reverend Donald Hallberg, president, ELCA Foundation and former Advocate Health Care board member; the Reverend Thomas Hurlocker, former president and CEO, Tressler Lutheran Services; Dan Mason, son of John M. Mason; Susan Myers, director, Lutheran Adoption Network; Joanne Negstad, past president and CEO, Lutheran Services in America; Mark Peterson, president and CEO, Lutheran Social Services of Minnesota; Dr. David Preus, former president, American Lutheran Church; James J. Raun, former president and CEO, Tressler Lutheran Services; Jill Schumann, president and CEO, Lutheran Services in America; the Reverend Kenneth Senft, retired executive, Division for Mission in North America, Lutheran Church in America; Jerry Wagenknecht, senior vice president of Mission and Spiritual Care, Advocate Health Care; the Reverend Greg Wilcox, vice president, Mission Effectiveness for Society.

2. "About Lutheran Services in America," http://www.lutheranservices.org.

3. "Introduction to Holt: A Historical Perspective," http://www.holtintl.org/historical.shtml; emphasis in original.

4. David Morstad, "Brief Histories of Bethesda Lutheran Homes and Services: 1940–1985," 2.

5. Richard W. Solberg, *Open Doors: The Story of Lutherans Resettling Refugees* (St. Louis: Concordia Publishing House, 1992), 28.

6. Ibid, 66.

7. Eric Sigmon, Suzie Lee, and Susan Yao, "LIRS Continues Comprehensive Immigration Reform Advocacy," *Advocacy Update* (July 2007), http://www.lirs.org/News/AdvoUpdate/Advo200707.html.

8. "LIRS's Mission, Vision and Values," http://www.lirs.org/who/mission.htm.

9. Fredric M. Norstad, *Presentations: Governance and Philosophy* (Park Ridge, IL: Lutheran General Health System, 1971), 5.

10. "Overview of Advocate," http://www.advocatehealth.com/system/about/overview.html.

11. Author's interview with staff of Appropriations Committee, Subcommittee on Labor, Health and Human Services, and Education, United States House of Representatives, 1992.

12. Ziegler Capital Markets Group, *2007 AAHSA Ziegler 100*; see PDFs of report, available at http://www.zieglerseniorlivingfinance.com/display/router.aspx?DocID=744.

13. Vision and mission statements are from "The Essentials of Lutheran Services in America," http://www.lutheranservices.org/Mission.asp.

14. Jill Schumann, "LSA Member Lutheran Social Ministry Organizations: Member Information, June 2007."

15. Author's interview with Mark Peterson, February 2008.

7. Where Do We Go from Here?

1. The following material was contributed by Jill Schumann, CEO/President, Lutheran Services in America, and used with her permission.

Index